DEATH

DEATH

From Dust to Destiny

Richard Brilliant

REAKTION BOOKS

IN MEMORIAM . . .

Published by Reaktion Books Ltd
Unit 32, Waterside
44–48 Wharf Road
London N1 7UX, UK
www.reaktionbooks.co.uk

First published 2017
Copyright © Richard Brilliant 2017

Printed and bound in China

A catalogue record for this book is available from the British Library

ISBN 978 1 78023 725 1

Contents

into the ground, with the addition of the symbolic shovelfuls of earth laid upon it at the bottom of the grave. Billy, once rambunctious Billy, was dead, and soon enough would be reduced to a memory among those assembled.

I remember now that I had tried to understand what 'being dead' meant and why the funeral seemed to be an attempt not only to affirm the fact of Billy's death, but to provide some opportunity for closure, befitting his brief, otherwise immature life. And I thought of myself as being young like Billy, without the guarantee of longevity, and wondered how that awareness might consciously shape my own life. At least, thinking about Billy's funeral – which was more than seventy years ago – I have come to realize that Billy's sudden death and the subsequent ceremonies stimulated me to observe and analyse the survivors' behaviour that followed. It was not a morbid preoccupation with death but, rather, with the perception of death and the varied experience of loss, which are subjected to ritual.

Despite the apparent finality of Billy's funeral, closure was still absent. Billy's immediate family never fully recovered from this death; an aura of perpetual sadness hovered over them, especially evident in his older brother and his father, my uncle. Whether or not it was because I was partly substitutional for Billy, I gradually drew closer to both of them.

Shortly after Billy's death my grandfather died after a long illness. I loved him dearly and was eager to accept the responsibility of serving as one of the pallbearers at his funeral. His burial seemed far different from Billy's; he was 78 and not fifteen, and had died so peacefully that his advanced age and its termination in the presence of his family brought us a satisfying, if reluctant, closure to his life.

The chronological connection between these two deaths and my participation in both funerals served to focus my interest in funerals, both in general and in their attendant ceremonies. I decided to learn more about funerals and the ceremonies surrounding them. I began to go to Catholic, Protestant, Jewish, Masonic and various ethnic funerals, scanning the obituary columns in the local newspapers for interesting opportunities. I did not know the deceased, and whenever possible I went to the funeral and to the post-funeral ceremonies at the home of the departed, especially to Irish homes, where the celebration of the wake created such a convivial atmosphere, with food and drink and good companionship, that death could hardly intrude. Unlike weddings, where a guest can be asked whether he/she belongs on the groom's or bride's side, at a wake no one asks who you are or why you have come; the family is happy to see you paying your respects to the deceased, and to them as well.

Sometimes, if I could obtain transportation, I also went to the cemetery, threw dirt on the gravesite if asked, and spoke kindly, if generally, about the dead person. I did this for about two years and then stopped because I began to feel that my presence was intrusive. However, the memory of these many funerals remained with me, often focused on the cemeteries, their resplendent grounds and the sepulchral monuments whose quiet appeal I responded to then, and now. Many of these cemeteries are conceived as arboreta, as if the flowering plants and trees stand as living witnesses to the cycle of life, complementing the monumental images and their aspirational inscriptions, promising to remember 'forever'.

IN RETROSPECT

YET I NEVER DID figure out how the dead could be 'resting', peacefully or otherwise, once buried. These old experiences have finally resolved themselves in this book about death and its effect on the living.

Some seventy years later, still thinking about death as a fitting subject of qualified response, I have long been collecting images, texts and the thoughts of concerned generations in this fundamental expression of self-awareness. Finally, in 2015, I set myself down to write the book long intended, fully appreciating the complexity of the deceased from death to an everlasting simulacrum of life in the afterlife of the 'Other World'.

The Egyptian *Book of the Dead* survives in a large number of illustrated manuscripts from the New Kingdom (*c.* 1550–1077 BCE) and later. They provide an instructive narrative for the deceased, detailing the relationship between the world of the living and the world of the (once) dead and how to effect the passage between them so that the transiting soul may continue to exist in an active state forever.[2] Personhood, sometimes identified as the *ba* or *ka*, an essential spirit of the deceased, was ill-defined but its ongoing existence was assumed if the necessary rituals were performed properly, even in the form of an apparition with little or no material substance. The jackal-headed god Anubis, deeply implicated in the Egyptian ritual and a central character in the *Book of the Dead*, became a familiar token of Egyptian mortuary ritual as well as an icon in its perennial imagery.

Thus the figure of Anubis, as guardian and gatekeeper of the honoured dead, was readily adaptable to Tony Fitzpatrick's highly political *Apparition of the Honored Chicago Dead* (2004), a sardonic, even sarcastic riff on the violent Democratic National Convention held in Chicago in 1968.[3] Mayor Richard J. Daley controlled admission to the convention hall and in so doing caused a dysfunctional spectacle with serious negative consequences for the Democratic presidential campaign, whose ultimate fate was then governed by Anubis. Anubis, characteristically presented in a New Kingdom papyrus, is depicted positively, receiving the mummified body of the deceased, Ani, into the netherworld; before the entrance into his tomb, Ani's kneeling widow, with a strong gesture of mourning, weeps.[4]

It is not only Anubis' image that resonates through the centuries, as an essential part of Egyptian sepulchral iconography. The architecture of Ani's tomb, with its pyramidal upper level resembling an obelisk, similarly endures as a conventionalized architectural topos, marking the immodest presence of an important tomb even in this reduced form. Lofty pyramidal elements on the upper levels of tombs became an ostentatious means of displaying wealth and power in various places in the ancient Mediterranean world, because the Egyptian precedent was so well known and visually salient in the landscape of that special siting.

The tombs in the Kidron Valley, near Jerusalem, exemplify this so-called usage and positioning, especially the Tomb of Zechariah.[5] The Tombs of the Maccabees near Modi'in, dated to the early second century BCE, must have been similar in purpose and ostentation:

'The Formal Farewell', from the Egyptian Papyrus of Ani, 19th dynasty.

Maccabean Tombs in the Kidron Valley, East Jerusalem.

He [Simon] also erected seven pyramids, opposite one
another, for his father and mother and four brothers. And
for the pyramids he devised an elaborate setting, erecting
about them great columns, and upon the columns he put
suits of armour for a permanent memorial, and beside the
suits of armour carved ships, so that they could be seen
by all who sail the sea.

I MACCABEES 13:28–9

The Maccabees had nothing to do with Egypt, despite the Egyptian
provenance of their tombs' design, but the Pyramid of Cestius, built
c. 18–12 BCE in Rome, located just outside the Porta San Paolo, is
strongly Egyptianized.[6] In Augustan Rome, an Egyptianizing style
became very fashionable, and Gaius Cestius, a wealthy, well-connected
Roman praetor, seems to have not only availed himself of contemporary fashion but assumed an Egyptian imagery of permanence,
expressed in its purest geometric form: a perfectly regular pyramid.[7]

Nestling beside Cestius' tomb lies the Protestant Cemetery of
Rome, containing in its verdant gardens the gravestones of John Keats

(1795–1821) and Percy Bysshe Shelley (1792–1822). Shelley's grave carries the following inscription taken from *The Tempest*:

> Nothing of him that doth fade,
> But doth suffer a sea-change
> Into something rich and strange.

The Romantic sentiment of this immortal English poet flourishes in the sequestered environment of the Protestant Cemetery, away from the bustle of modern Rome and its Catholic cemeteries. Shelley was a noble foreigner in a strange land whose poetic journey of discovery only seems to have ended beside Cestius' unique tomb, as if he were drawing inspiration from its interruptive, isolated presence. Furthermore, such a prominent and distinctive monument had the power to draw attention to itself as a magnet for other sepulchral monuments, which in turn gain prestige and, potentially, an audience in attendance upon them.

The Pyramidal Tomb of Gaius Cestius, near the Porta San Paolo, Rome, 1st century BCE.

Oklahoma City National Memorial, designed by Hans and Torrey Butzer.

Stalin have been torn down. All over the country, wherever statues were thus destroyed, Lenin statues have sprung up by the thousands. They grow like weeds on the ruins, like melancholy flowers of forgetting.[19]

Some cultural ghosts reappear suddenly in the midst of nowhere; some by chance, others by intention. Chinese archaeologists have excavated a four-thousand-year-old cemetery in the desert of Xinjiang, near the ancient East–West Silk Road. The mummified dead have European features and long noses and were buried in upside-down boats; their DNA is indicative of Siberian and European ancestry, not of peoples native to the area. The cemetery is marked even now by a forest of phallic symbols, carved on logs set upright, very prominent in this bare environment.[20]

'The Aboriginal Memorial consists of an installation of 200 hollow log coffins from Central Arnhem Land commemorating all the indigenous people who, since 1788, have lost their lives defending their land.' So reads the statement of the National Gallery of Australia in Canberra, where these log coffins stand presently on display. Inspired by a new political climate in Australia which revalued its Aboriginal population, the memorial was created by Aboriginal artists in the 1980s not just as a testament to the vitality of their own culture but as a cenotaphic monument to their many dead in Arnhem Land – the memorialization and reaffirmation of the independent value of *their* continuous presence in *their* ancient land. Indeed, the very idea of the 'Aboriginal' suggests a priority of possession, projected into the present by living survivors: Australian nationals.

Unnamed Lands

Nations ten thousand years before these States, and many
    times ten thousand years before these States,
Garner'd clusters of ages, that men and women like us
    grew up and travel'd their course, and pass'd on,

What vaſt-built cities, what orderly republics, what
    paſtoral tribes and nomads,

What hiſtories, rulers, heroes, perhaps transcending all
    others,

What laws, cuſtoms, wealth, arts, traditions,

What sort of marriage, what coſtumes, what physiology
    and phrenology,

What of liberty and slavery among them, what they
    thought of death and the soul,

Who were witty and wise, who beautiful and poetic, who
    brutish and undevelop'd,

Not a mark, not a record remains – and yet all remains.

WALT WHITMAN, *Leaves of Grass* (1855)

of the passer-by, who would see, stop, and read the inscribed text (one hoped).

The inscription asserts certain states of belief: non-existence before birth, and again at the end of life. The succinctness of this life story, wrapped in a mantle of indifference, seems undermined by the very statement, its mode of presentation and by the presence of 'the speaker' in the linguistic form of expression. The self-serving 'I' in the text exists as a counter-assertive presence, even as a reiteration of that presence – four times in the inscription.

Once read as intended, the deceased enters into a dialogue with the reader that is the essence of this form of sepulchral communication. At the very least, this individual wanted to be remembered as non-caring, possibly as an indication either of modesty or being unafraid of death. Furthermore, the syntactic contrast between the perfect state of the past tense *fui* and the unlimited presentness of a persistent exist-ence – *non curo* – suggests a more complicated, deeper meaning. The unbounded statement implies an obdurate, even confident image of the deceased, subject, in turn, to an extended interpretation by the reader.[2]

The presence of the reader, of any reader of this sepulchral text and its specific formulation, precludes the possibility of complete closure,[3] endowing the otherwise absent deceased with an active presence in the reader's mind: 'he does not care, so should I?' Invocation is a constant of Roman epitaphic inscriptions, seen in the many thousands of Roman funerary reliefs directly addressed to the sacred spirits of the dead – *Dis manibus sacrum*.[4] Calling up the spirits of the dead expresses a pious belief in their propitiatory role in death rituals but does not expect the reappearance of the dead, nor that survivors who pass by be patient readers. Rather, this formulaic invocation preceded, usually, a series of brief notes from the dead to the living. These involved various beliefs regarding immortality, the underworld, the 'sleep' of the dead, efforts of consolation, biographical themes and, often, practical references, stressing the contribution of family members, friends and former servants to the cost of the tomb.[5] These texts were also often very formulaic, given the limited literacy of most of the contemporary public, but the formulas were so familiar, so omnipresent in cemeteries, that their meaning would be immediately accessible to a range of persons.

A closer look at this extensive epigraphic culture, with its tradition of providing the names of the dead, often accompanied by a portrait and the age at death, exposes the biographical particulars of the past life to view. By this means, the deceased is extricated from the commonplace oblivion of death. The funerary monument exhibiting such details serves as a surrogate for the life once lived and a bulwark against forgetting.[6]

Inscribed Egyptian funerary stele of Kherituankh, 2nd century BCE.

This ancient commemorative apparatus, associating monument and memory, retained its authority for centuries, and was acknowledged by St Augustine in his *De cura pro mortuis gerenda* (On Care to be Had for the Dead), written around 421. It perseveres in the inscription of a funerary slab in the Palisades Cemetery near New York City:

ISAAC D. TALLMAN

ENGINEER

Was killed on the

N.Y. & E. RR

While running the night express

ENGINE NO. 37

Caused by a rock laying on the track

April 4, 1853

Aged 30 years, 3 months

and 26 days[7]

Some of the details may seem trivial but they never are for the deceased or for those who knew him.

There were larger funerary inscriptions in the ancient world which constituted in themselves manifestations of an intrinsic monumentality that also made presumptions on the extended attention span of an individual exposed to them in the public space.[8] A primary example of such a monumental inscription comes from the Mausoleum of the Flavii at Cilium (at Kasserine, Tunisia), where it is endowed with an elaborate poetic form:

> Yes, life is very short and its moments fleeting, our days torn from us pass like a brief hour, our mortal bodies are drawn deep down in to the Elysian Fields by malevolent Lachesis bent on cutting the skein of our lives ... Memory, made less ephemeral, collects them and keeps many

souvenirs: inscriptions are made so that the years endure ... Who henceforth could ſtop here without feeling a rush of virtue, who would not admire this maſterpiece, who, on seeing this profusion of riches, would not remain thunderſtruck before the immense resources that have enabled this monument to be projeċted into the ether? This is the moſt honourable way of using one's fortune, it is thus that spending one's money procures imperishable dwelling places.

... I don't doubt that in the silent darkness of Acheron, if the dead ſtill have feelings, your father muſt often feel joy, Secundus, and look down on the battalion of the other shades, for he knows that here his tomb continues to exiſt, eternally new in all its majeſty, that these ſtones, perfeċtly matched, rise up in all their splendour, that rising from their foundation these tall buildings have seen their beauty grow to such an extent that each of these ridges seems marked out perfeċtly ſtraight in soft wax. From the movement of the ſtatues the sculptor's art brings into being a new charm; and the crowd of passers-by can without wearying admire these splendours and marvel to see the harmonious balance of the columns shining above their heads. Furthermore you offered to the gods the inscription of the ſtates of service of your father, and your father in person.

... Now is the time to maintain that your father is immortal, that he has left behind Dis and fled its siniſter palace, since he prefers, until the end of time, to follow the fate of this monument and live, thanks to these names inscribed here eternally ...

... a monument for the future.[9]

This monument resiſts the passage of time and the forgetting and ruin which come with it. And what is that monument other than a highly visible presence, its prominence assured by size and embellishment, which assure survival. By these means, the Monument of the Flavii actively projects into future memories the record of a distinguished man and the piety of those who honoured him. Subsequent encounters with this monument elicit freshened memories, inevitably changed from their originating sources because of the passage of time, but not completely. The Flavii at Cilium are represented as being worthy of remembrance, given that they were once commemorated – so the standing monument reminds the viewer/reader.[10]

The encomium of the Flavii embedded in the inscription derives from the Roman oral tradition of the eulogy, made permanent in stone. A similar sepulchral inscription in honour of Quintus Veranius, consular in 49 CE, also survives, displaying the rhetorical flourishes and personal, historical matters typical of this genre.[11] Roman eulogies, or *laudationes funebres*, survive in only fragmented texts, despite their importance to distinguished honourees and their families. These eulogistic texts emphasize family and ancestors, the decedent's achievements and experiences, and their virtue, all wrapped up in established formulas of praise.[12] The irony in Mark Antony's funeral oration for Julius Caesar in Shakespeare's play is bitterly evident, beginning with the famous lines:

> Friends, Romans, countrymen, lend me your ears;
> I come to bury Caesar, not to praise him.
> The evil that men do lives after them;
> The good is oft interred with their bones;
> So let it be with Caesar.
> (Act III, Scene 2)

Antony goes on to identify Caesar's many virtuous acts and the wrongs done to him, repeating Caesar's name more than twenty times. Those in the audience during the delivery of this impassioned speech can imagine Caesar's spirit nodding approval at each mention of his name. The familiar wish to live long enough to hear what people have to say at one's funeral is a common, if frustrated, ambition, reflecting the strength of vanity.

Few loom like buried Caesar in the minds of his public, his friends and his many subsequent admirers. Thus, if they find distinction, the destinction mentioned in funeral monuments depends on other forms of respect: Erasmus of Rotterdam, the great humanist who died in 1536, is celebrated for his incomparable erudition and scholarship in his inscribed grave stele, presently located in Basel Minster; Frances Palmer, the faithful and loving wife of one Edward Palmer, died in childbirth in 1628 and was commemorated by an elaborately inscribed

Inscribed grave stele of Erasmus of Rotterdam, Basel Minster, early 16th century.

monument at Stoke Doyle, Northamptonshire, which showed her bidding farewell to her husband and surviving children.[13]

Erasmus, a servant of Christ, enjoyed worldwide fame not just for his scholarship but for his virtuous character; Frances Palmer epitomized in her life the modest, virtuous wife and mother. The quality of their respective virtue cannot be measured, perhaps because it represents a state of goodness that is absolute without reference to the scale of reputation. Still, Palmer's monument, its dependence on family life and her reception by her husband and children, lies close to the normative expressions of loss and commemoration, offset by the ribbons of obituary notices printed in today's daily newspapers, encomiums of praiseworthy acts.

Obituaries track lives, sometimes in excruciating detail, sometimes at extended, costly length; sometimes supplemented with photographs of the recently deceased, sometimes filled with the names of close relatives and friends; sometimes with the notice of the time and place of the funeral, and of the cemetery where 'the remains will be laid to rest', and sometimes with suggestions of where contributions in memoriam can be sent. Of course, celebrities and the 'famous' have the benefit of larger articles in the press, the result of archival collections prepared in advance and written by staff journalists, conscious of their contribution to the historical record. But most modern obituaries, often paid for by relatives or by associations long connected with the deceased, are produced by practised writers assigned to the task; they begin, usually, with the full name of the deceased and the date of death, then follow with the biographical details provided by family members and chosen to enhance the stature of the deceased as much as possible. A wide readership exists for these obituaries, and this, coupled with the sizeable circulation of newspapers and journals, provides a much greater opportunity to achieve public notice than ever before. The modern scope of the 'death beat' for journalists assigned to writing obituaries may be new, but the themes and topics related have a very long tradition behind them, indicating the persistence of values imputed to the dead and of the ritualized foundations of commemoration. Woe betide any obituarist who fails to do right by the deceased, as if the insult could lead to their premature resurrection in vengeance.[14]

Given the itemized particulars common to obituaries, the question remains of what can be omitted from the representational agenda without compromising the commemorative programme and obscuring its special reference to an honoured individual. The cover of the *New Yorker* from 18 January 1999 bears biographically explicit imagery detailing important episodes in the life and death of Martin Luther King. Compartmentalized in the manner of medieval manuscript illumination, the cover constitutes, in effect, a visual obituary, monumentalized by the artist Edward Sorel. The ensemble of elements traces a historical progression from birth to death, ending not in a death scene but in a symbolic gravestone, engraved with words sacralized by King himself, expressing his true aspiration.

Despite these words, associated closely with Martin Luther King, and the three familiar images of the well-known honouree, his name never appears. It is assumed that the identity of this famous protagonist, the advocate of racial justice, this great-hearted man, would be so familiar to the magazine's readership that no name would be needed to complete his identification. Of course, the *New Yorker* cover looks like a monument, but it is not. Perhaps fifty years from now the celebrated referent would not be identified.

Names, personal names, are central to celebratory commissions because they establish the bedrock of the commemorative agenda by focusing attention on the human agent. A simple wall plaque in Rome commemorates the death of Remo Perpetua, one of the victims of the German reprisal in March 1944 when more than three hundred Roman citizens, many of them Jews, were taken from the Via Rasella near the Palazzo Barberini in Rome and murdered. Their bodies were secretly buried by the Germans in the Ardeatine caves on the outskirts of Rome; their remains were later found, and these victims

A fan of Frankie Manning, standing before his tombstone
in Woodlawn Cemetery, the Bronx, New York.

Speaking with the dead may appear to be one-sided, unless a tomb's inscription invites dialogue, a responsive reading. People often buy cemetery plots to be buried near their relatives, preserving family units, friends for old time's sake, and famous persons, even strangers whom they adore. One Victor Gaines bought such a plot in Woodlawn Cemetery in New York City to be close to Duke Ellington and Frankie Manning, and seems to be addressing the latter in his visit.[24] Personalized headstones encourage such connections, especially when the person represented seems to face the visitor directly.

Such active grave markers make a spirited claim to an ongoing place in the world. There is a conceived expectation that the living visitor and the dead can meet and establish more than a one-way exchange. The desire to speak with the dead, and for the dead to speak to the living, seems to respond to the felt desire to collapse time, to open the gates to the past, a past once shared.[25]

The 'dead' are a great army, still on the march; their numbers are constantly growing, their tombs and sepulchral monuments encroaching on open land. Today, these large, expanding communities of the dead frame the urban centres of the West and line the exurban highways, connecting them, as stark reminders of human destiny. Although many modern cemeteries are green, embellished by flowering shrubs and trees in season, their landscapes are punctuated by pale stone monuments, often ghostly white, like the shades of the dead whose presence is so deliberately marked, especially in winter.[26] To think of these cemeteries as 'final resting places' would seem delusional, given the constant activity of burial, religiously inspired visits and the talkative movement of curious tourists, drawn to the celebrity of some of the inhabitants.

After the passage of years, plain gravestones, if they are still standing, and even grand sepulchral monuments tend to lose their once attentive public. The names of the dead whose inscriptions survive

Silk embroidered memorial, early 19th century.

preserve some individuating particularity for the living as an ultimate possession, an indexical mark of a former existence. There is an old superstition that one should never call out the dead by name, lest they or their spirits be called up.[27] Perhaps that is a good reason for silent behaviour in a cemetery, beyond that of traditional respect, lest the dead answer to their stated name – surely an indication of their posthumous power.

Death is universal and completely democratic; it happens to us all. Many cemeteries, however, restrict admissions for burial according to varying criteria: religion, ethnic culture, social class, civil status, occupation, prior family presence, degree of wealth, political and institutional connections, philanthropic, scientific or artistic reputation, and race. These discriminative criteria, controlling admission to the

St Andrew's Church, Staten Island, New York, in winter.

Roman family grave stele, 2nd century CE, Archaeological Museum, Zagreb.

Detail of a mosaic tomb slab, Early Christian burial complex, Leptiminus, Tunisia, 5th century.

hallowed ground, shape the buried population of cemeteries, but the possession or absence of virtue is usually not among them.[28]

Close family relationships have always been important, especially the nuclear family, involving parents and their children since Roman antiquity.[29] When the family has dynastic connections, the membership of generations and their entrance into a common tomb appears to be the norm. So it was with the family of King Abgar of Edessa (first century CE), whose family tomb in southeastern Turkey portrays family members as busts in a mosaic, dominated by the central, larger figure of the king himself.[30] The impulse is towards collectivity, the strengthening of the deceased individual through association with others: families with offspring, husbands and wives, and co-religionists. Collectivity reinforces group identity in a social milieu; it draws greater and more frequent attendance, thereby enhancing the experience of each in the context of all, and is therefore one of the motivations for the creation of cemeteries and in the related gathering of funerary monuments along a street lined with tombs, like the Via Appia outside Rome, the Via delle Tombe at Pompeii,[31] or the zone around San Lorenzo in Rome. Systematic mortuary display, joining elements of individual sepulchral monuments in a singular field of space and vision, is not restricted to exterior spaces but is a familiar element of sepulchral dynamics within or beside religious structures, in church interiors and on extended church grounds, bringing together the burial rite, the monument and the commemorative anniversary in one place, where memory and its periodic reactivation can best take hold.[32]

Complementary interaction among those elements that posit heroic or mythic models as a vehicle for the elevation of the deceased to some higher plane is at work in the collection of pagan Roman sarcophagi, reused in the Middle Ages and Renaissance for Christian burials. A fine example of this adaptive process is to be found in the adaptation of a Phaedra and Hippolytus sarcophagus in the Camposanto in Pisa, used for reburial in 1576, an act recorded in the inscription

Roman Hippolytus sarcophagus converted into a Renaissance tomb,
Camposanto, Pisa, 1576.

(translated): 'Although I am a sinner, called Miſtress Beatrice, put
forth in the tomb, I lie [here] as any Countess'. Whether the deceased
Beatrice was aware of the significance of the mythological sarcophagus
in which she was buried, the recognizably antique source was itself
sufficient to ennoble the casket containing her body, as well as herself.
The Camposanto is filled with *spolia*; for centuries numerous Roman
mythological sarcophagi were used with little or no change for the
caskets for Chriſtian dignitaries. The apparent irrelevance of the
ancient mythological subjeĉt did not seem to matter, when an elaborately sculpted work served to enhance the beauty and visual authority
of a medieval or Renaissance tomb. The contraſt between such richly
sculpted caskets, held clearly above ground to be highly visible, and
the flat tomb slabs set in the floor of Italian cathedrals muſt have been
readily observed, at firſt.

Tomb of Tomasso
Sacchetti (d. 1404)
set in the floor of
Santa Croce, Florence.

Their apparent modesty was in keeping with the contemporary traditions of Christian piety, a tradition that continued to repress the monumental impulse, but not always. Grandiose, elaborately sculpted tombs began to appear in public areas or inserted into the pre-existing walls of churches in Italy from Naples to Milan and Verona, in royal centres in France, Germany and England, where they constituted an ostentatious display of pride and power.[33] Humbler tomb slabs, set in the floors of churches, were subject to foot passage and did not wear very well. The resulting erosion of the sepulchral image and of its accompanying inscriptions seriously compromised the effectiveness of the original commemorative intent, but was nonetheless evocative of Christian humility.

Not so the thousands of Roman upright, standing sepulchral grave monuments, which offered an unprecedented array of 'ordinary' individuals, their identities complete with named inscriptions, portraits of themselves and family members, and their occupations, all carefully carved into the face of their sepulchral monument. These popular grave monuments record for posterity members of the Roman 'middle class' – persons of some status, modest wealth and social position who considered themselves worthy of notice and were willing to pay for it. The demographic, social and territorial range is vast: witness the cenotaphic gravestones of Marcus Caelius, a soldier on the Rhine frontier killed in 9 BCE, in Bonn, who displays his many military decorations; of Gallo-Roman bankers in central France; the Secundinii, cloth merchants in Trier; Ravennate shipbuilders; a potter and his wife from Italy; a theatrical company of actors; the Haterii, in the construction business; a circus master; slave traders in Amphipolis in the Roman East; and the baker Eurysaces, whose grand monument beside the Porta Maggiore in Rome brought attention to his role as an industrial-scale baker for Caesar's army, the source of his fortune.[34] Merchants, bankers, traders, wine shippers and artisans these Romans were – a class in the middle that did not rise again to prominence for more than a millennium.

The urge to be remembered was so strong that even in the darkness of the subterranean Roman catacombs efforts were made to be noticed. Bodies of the dead, shrouded, were placed in narrow, horizontal slits cut in the natural stone walls along the passageways; these slits, called *loculi*, were often closed by plaques of marble bearing the names of the deceased. Sometimes these plaques were more elaborate, their inscriptions more elegantly drawn; so it is with the early Christian burial of one Procla in a catacomb off the Via Anapo in Rome, where an inscription of high quality is flanked by supportive winged genii.

of these larger chambers within the catacomb may also hold some burials, but they are not primarily tombs but rather sacred spaces where rituals and prayers would take place under a canopy bearing strong eschatological messages to believers. Subterranean catacombs occupy the same zone beneath the surface of the earth into which most burials enter. Yet late Roman communities – pagan, Jewish and Christian – made an effort to alleviate the cloak of darkness by the lightness of the intermittent painted chambers and by the names and religious symbols engraved on the plaques fronting the *loculi*.

'Stay, look, discover and engage' with the final resting place of a known deceased; these admonitions together constitute the common instruction to the passer-by in the ancient gravesites. How disappointing or disillusioning must be the experience of a more recent graveyard, above ground, where the shadows of the night and the erosion of time have so completely obscured the identities of the deceased.[36] Even more, the vast necropolis of the dead in the Great War must numb the mind despite the names inscribed on the seried tombstones. The British Commonwealth Cemetery near Ypres, Belgium, contains the graves of nearly 13,000 soldiers; more than 8,000 of them are, however,

View of a decaying 19th-century cemetery in Connecticut.

British Commonwealth Cemetery in Tyne Cot, Belgium, near Ypres,
the site of a great, deadly battle.

identified only as 'A Soldier of the Great War, Known Unto God'.[37]
That secret is still kept.

Anonymity, the fall into neglect of abandoned cemeteries, or burial
in unmarked graves in a potter's field, block the attempts of would-be
mourners to visit their dead, to find a fitting ending to an undetermined
memory. Remembering and mourning seem to go together, a means of
reconciling past and present in a close bond of activated relationships.
This bond is appropriate to the commemorative reception of the dead
but also contributes to the living's sense of their own mortality. The
almost numberless victims of the Holocaust so often left no remains,
and no relatives and friends, that the opportunity to attach specific
memories to individuals has been impaired, unless combined within
the sombre aggregate of the Holocaust memorial.[38]

Genocide leaves terrible scars. Those same scars and a poignant
awareness of the 'missing' energize the actions and feelings of self-aware

cultures is evidence of the ambiguity of this semi-final relationship, expressing the tension between adhesion and withdrawal. Typically, these rites are replete with admonitions about pollution, the potential contamination of and by the interred, the need to placate the 'spirit' of the dead to ensure their posthumous existence in the 'other world', and other requirements directed to the obligation of the living towards the dead; performance seems to be at least partly a means of self-protection.[7] Certainly, a dramatic resolution of this tension concludes Peter Nádas's play *Burial* (1982), when the principal actor, the lone presence on the stage, closes himself in his coffin.[8]

Between the dying and those in attendance thereupon, an exchange of 'farewells' may often occur. These are fairly one-sided, one should say, because only one party is leaving (life), as in this poem by Wallace Stevens:

> Between farewell and the absence of farewell,
> The final mercy and the final loss,
> The wind and the sudden falling of the wind.[9]

Reciprocating 'farewells' are common in many languages and cultures, when both parties are equivalent and, potentially, cannot meet again unless there is an anticipated encounter in the afterlife, as some would have it; meeting again in the normal course of life is unlikely when one party is deceased. As Jacques Derrida would prefer to imagine, because of the deep memory of the departed, the memory image undergoes an active interiorization. As a result, the departed never fully become absent, remaining so within the survivor, in effect incorporated into the other self, that the affective bonds of friendship never break.[10]

The integrative forces of affection and memory powerfully bind together the living and dead in an ongoing relationship. The intimacy so realized, however, remains a fictive reality; one may embrace an idea, a dream or a memory image, but these are immaterial, the last the ghost of an individual lost to death who no longer lives in the world but has not suffered oblivion, because he is *missed*.

The poignancy of this relationship informs a mid-nineteenth-century gravestone in a New York cemetery which displays the necessary ingredients of a concentrated obituary: the name of the deceased, the date of his death, his age at death, his paramount faith in God, his patriotism, symbolized by the American eagle, and his membership in the Masonic order, indicated by the all-seeing eye.[11] Like some well-realized character in a Dickens novel, Daniel Clark had a richly detailed, memorable existence once, but he is no more. That separation, effected by death on 6 September 1856, has been duly acknowledged by the standing gravestone. And yet, a small inscription at the foot of the gravestone has been inserted in a less formal style.

Daniel Clark's tombstone, *c.* 1856, New York City.

It states, 'Father, we miss thee'. This mode of very direct address, expressed by Clark's children, conveys their wish to communicate directly to him, as if he could hear them, as if they could still speak to him directly. Clark is both *missed* and *missing*, lost to life but not to them. They, his survivors, continue to feel the emotional pangs of grief. The connection between the two poles of loss – his and theirs – can be achieved through personal and ritual mourning, whereby Clark's children may be able to adjust to his absence, to being left behind.[12]

For some individuals, this adjustment is very difficult. Reiterated episodes of mourning punctuate their daily lives, stimulated by fragments of memory attached to familiar things. So it was with Emily Dickinson:

> Death sets a Thing significant
> The Eye had hurried by
> Except a perished Creature
> Entreat us tenderly
>
> To ponder little Workmanships
> In Crayon, or in Wool,
> With 'This was last Her fingers did' –
> Industrious until –
>
> The Thimble weighed too heavy –
> The stitches stopped – themselves –
> And then 'twas put among the Dust
> Upon the Closet shelves –
>
> A Book I have – a friend gave –
> Whose Pencil – here and there –
> Had notched the place that pleased Him –
> At Rest – His fingers are –

Now – when I read – I read not –
For interrupting Tears –
Obliterate the Etchings
Too Costly for Repairs.[13]

For others, like Paul Celan, the magnitude of personal loss coupled with the enormity of the Holocaust brought forth dirge-like poems of death, such as 'Todesfuge' (Death Fugue, 1944–5), which begins with the line 'Black milk of daybreak we drink', repeated with variations like a refrain.[14] The poet's juxtaposition of 'black' and 'milk', the one a conscious symbol of mourning, the other a life-giving fluid, establishes their polarity within the span of day that stands for the course of life, a tragic life itself. This temporal imagery seems to echo a precedent in Ecclesiastes 7:

A good name is better than precious ointment; and the
day of death than the day of birth.
It is better to go to the house of mourning, than to go
to the house of feasting; for that is the end of all
men, and the living will lay it to his heart.
Sorrow is better than laughter, for by sadness of countenance the heart is made glad.
The heart of the wise is in the house of mourning; but
the heart of fools is in the house of mirth.

Celan's invocation of black relies on the symbolic colour of mourning, customary in many societies. In southern Italy widows wear black the rest of their lives, as did Queen Victoria following the death of Prince Albert, and black is the ultimate negation of the living in Sol LeWitt's *Black Form: Dedicated to the Missing Jews* in Hamburg, discussed earlier. Black also permeates the compound memorial to the murdered President J. F. Kennedy, the Reverend Martin Luther King and Senator Robert Kennedy, grouped in a visceral souvenir of their association designed by Kerry James Marshall in 1997. Accents of sombre blackness are everywhere here: plants and flowers are black; the central space is occupied by a winged figure, dressed in black from head to toe, like an Angel of Death who seems to look out at the viewer as if to include them, sooner or later. In the firmament, above, hovering in the clouds of memory, the heads of other dearly departed loom like disembodied spirits, as if waiting for the death bell to toll, to welcome others into a funeral parlour.

Prince Albert died in 1861 of natural causes, and his spouse, Queen Victoria, initiated a pervasive cult of mourning.[15] Because of her position, Victoria's comportment as a mourner, her dark clothing and her semi-reclusion from affairs became influential models, even standards of righteous behaviour, as if the feeling of loss could never end. She seemed to live with grief, never escaping from the stages of grief long studied by Elizabeth Kübler-Ross, who establishes the signs of Grief Disorder, defined in the fifth edition of the *Diagnostic and Statistical Manual of Mental Disorders* (2013): confusion about one's role in life, difficulty in accepting the loss, inability to trust others and other problems in engaging with life lasting for months or longer.

Victoria's behaviour soon diffused through American society of the 1860s, when an all-consuming culture of death – good or bad – took over, in response to the vast number of young men killed in the Civil War 'before their time'. Many died unattended on the battlefield, their anonymous graves thrown together in mass burials, unmarked.[16] Vast cemeteries proliferated to contain the bodies of the honoured dead; terms of mourning extended, responding to the scale of the killing and to the disappearance of so many who had gone to war and never returned, their final resting place forever unknown. The level of carnage, the terrible scale of dying and the fragmentation of bodies were unprec-edented. They would occur again in the First and Second World Wars, by which time people seemed to be more inured to the experience of massive loss of life, except following the bombings of Hiroshima and

Nagasaki, where tens of thousands of people disappeared in an instant, leaving behind neither bodies nor mourners.

The act of mourning, however expressed, requires the presence of active mourners, as a matter of practical necessity. They may be self-conscious mourners, sensible of their mediating place between a lost past and a socially responsible present, especially when that loss is monumentally realized, in effect a testament for the future. There exist well-established public and private mourning scenarios, and separate protocols for each, some of them highly ritualized. On Daniel Clark's tombstone the engraved statement that his children miss him is a sign both of their emotional response to his loss and of its continuity after death, considering the time it took to complete the tombstone, include the date of death and their message of grief – all for public notice.

The suffering inflicted on someone by the death of another who is or was close has fewer limits of time and deeper feelings of loss. These feelings are often difficult to express to oneself, as well as to others. Even established authors, skilled in the depiction of characters and behaviour, can find the burden of self-expression very painful when trying to discover the language needed to present their painful loss, while exposing themselves to their readers as mourners, and thus, vulnerable. In his *A Grief Observed* (1961), C. S. Lewis, long unmarried, mourned the early death of his vibrant young wife; Joan Didion, in *The Year of Magical Thinking* (2005), revealed the painful experience of her husband's illness and death, reflecting on her attempt to work through the process of mourning and acceptance.

Marital and other family relationships, broken by death, are not the only preconditions for eliciting the symptoms of deep mourning. Jacques Derrida's extended meditation on the death of his friend Emmanuel Levinas led to his composition of *The Work of Mourning* (1981–98), a profound response to that death and its aftermath. He felt such a strong intellectual bond that even Levinas's death could not break it, so intertwined were their lives and thoughts. All of these reflections, presented as personal experiences offered for literary consumption by others, challenge conventional notions that recovery from such losses is of short duration and can fairly quickly lead to an effective closure.[17]

The periodization of stages of mourning developed by some religions, such as Judaism, set out the day of death, the almost immediate burial, then the week, the month, the year and the anniversary. These moments lead eventually to the lessening of active grief and to the conflation of mourning and commemoration.

Mourning itself, as a distinct experience, becomes submerged into memorial because of the increasing distance from the fatal event. With the aid of modern technology such as Facebook, survivors can experience a biographical, pictorial scan of a departed life, a surrogate available for constant repetition as a means of reanimating the deceased before one's eyes. This surrogate may not, however, avoid restimulating the experience of grief once more, because the freshening of memory through images may only serve to confirm that the life depicted has ended. The re-experiencing of grief thereby elicited may be expressed as a verbal counterpart in the form of a lamentation.[18]

It is not easy to bring such sorrow to a satisfactory conclusion, even when there seems to be some way to compose oneself physically and emotionally, while reminiscing about the deceased when alive. Possibly, such willed delusion is even less available to any parent who mourns the death of a child, an all too familiar experience of loss, shaped but not limited by the specifics of cultural differences. Thus, from a tombstone near Mecca, dating from the tenth or eleventh century:

> Each day death unfurls its shroud
> and yet we persist, heedless of what awaits us . . .
> Where are the ones who were our comfort?
> Death made them drink the impure cup
> They have become captives under the heaped ground.[19]

From Marcus Cornelius Fronto, to 'My Lord M. Aurelius Antoninus', on the death of his grandson, 165 CE (partly quoted):

My lord, have you some words,
Some maxim of philosophy
To comfort your old rhetorician
And his grief-stricken family?

My daughter's only son,
My one grandson, age three,
Dear darling Decimanus,
To bed forever, so early.

He was as blond, as blue as –
But similes fail me.
What can Reason avail me
For such a loss, my lord?

The child Decimanus is dead.
Can an old man endure?
If I were of iron,
I could write not more.[20]

Of the children's memorial of the many, many Jewish children slaughtered during the Holocaust, now remembered at Yad Vashem, Philip Schultz wrote:

Inside a domed room photos of children's faces
turn in a candlelit dark as recorded voices
recite their names, ages and nationality.
'Ah, such beautiful faces,' a woman sighs.
Yes, but faces without the prestige
of the future or the tolerance of the past.
Not one asks: Why is this happening to me?
They stare at the camera as if it were a commandment:
thou shall not bear false witness . . .

. . .

We look at their faces and their faces look at us.

They know we are pious.

They know we grieve.

But they also know we will soon leave.

We are not their mothers and fathers,

who also could not save them.[21]

On 14 December 2012 twenty first-graders at a school in Newtown, Connecticut, were killed by a lone gunman. Their murder led to an outpouring of grief, sympathy and offerings of money and toys, but the important follow-up effort at gun control failed. There seems to be an unending list of the slaughter of children in modern times, as if killing the future, otherwise embodied in these children, were the desired goal of their premature deaths. For most, the death of a child is especially hard because there is so little recourse, so curtailed is the narrative of the child's life. For the elderly, grief is hard to bear because there are so many in one's age group dying, so many life stories coming to an end, such a shrinkage in one's age category.[22]

For the elderly, or for the chronically ill, the threat to one's own sense of fragile mortality is heightened by the death of contemporaries; their lives, too, had an imminent, if temporally unfixed, ending, and we prefer such endings for ourselves. Wallace Stevens's poem 'The Owl in the Sarcophagus' (1947) was written as an elegy to his friend Denny Church, when both were 68 years old. The poem is saturated with feelings of loss and with a reluctance to grasp that with the finality of death their biographies and his poetry would be silent. Yet, eight years later in 1955, perhaps less immediately pressed by Church's death, Stevens wrote 'A Clear Day and No Memories', which states that the poet has 'no thoughts of people now dead', as if he were turning away from a once remembered grief and had found clarity in the uncaring natural world.[23]

One way to be reconciled to our own death is to accept its certainty with equanimity, because we have no choice in the matter: 'Death sets a Thing significant', runs Emily Dickinson's arresting line. Memoirs of a parent by a child or by a surviving spouse, or of a child by a parent constitute a touching genre in which the identity of both the writer and the memorialized subject have been shaped by the sense of loss.[24] Whether that sense of loss is without remedy depends on the degree of separation of the writer from the deceased, attained in the very act of writing and in the value attributed to the life once lived, now rehearsed in the telling.

Mourning expressed in a variety of modes as grief over the loss of loved ones has permeated human cultures for millennia. Other species, such as elephants, apes, dogs, cats and even dolphins mourn, and do so recognizably, through downcast facial expressions, lowered tone of voice, tears and slumping body postures.[25] Such perceptible acts, expressions of grief, especially strong in the presence of the corpse,

Thomas Rowlandson, *Mourning Figures around a Coffin, c.* 1800, pen and ink with wash.

Stephen Greene, *The Mourners*, *c.* 1946, oil on canvas.

are not self-contained. They advertise the death of someone close to the principal sufferers to other members of their social group as a communal experience to be shared, and as a means of eliciting an empathetic response.[26]

An oil painting by the twentieth-century American artist Stephen Greene entitled *The Mourners* (*c.* 1946) displays the figures of three mourners against a backdrop of three wooden crosses. The Crucifixion of Christ and his two companions on Mount Calvary, a long icono-graphic model, has clearly been invoked, coupled with social commentary related pictorially to the work of the artist Ben Shahn, a contemporary of Greene, who was sensitive to social and political issues. The picture frame cuts off the top of the central cross, as if to indicate Christ's salvation, further implied by the ghostly, celestial figure in the upper left which directs its motion both towards the cross and to the male figure below. That figure, in turn, is dressed in the striped clothing of a concentration camp survivor, perhaps one recently liberated, given the date the painting was done. All three figures gesticulate, expressing their supplication, their sadness, but the central figure seems to be speaking perhaps to his invisible saviour.

The combination of gesticulating expressions of mourning and supplication has a long tradition in representational art, going back to ancient Egypt.[27] Other examples are to be found in ancient Paestan tomb paintings; in Roman wall paintings, represented by the 'Sacrifice of Iphigenia' in the House of the Tragic Poet in Pompeii; in late Burgundian tombs; and in Roman sarcophagi responding, appropriately, to the death of Meleager and the funeral of Hector, both in the Louvre.[28] Single-figure extractions from this repertory appear in figurines of a crying mourner from Maroitic Nubia, of Isis or Nephthys from the New Kingdom of Egypt, or the much later marble sculpture of the *Penitent Magdalene* by Antonio Canova. These oft-repeated figural types are generic, seeming to transcend any particular cultural system as normative modes of mournful expression, readily recognized in their self-imposed contortions.

There is something about this persistent imagery that bespeaks performance. Professional mourners have long been employed in many societies, as if in their cries, tears, torn clothing, untamed hair and

Opening of the Mouth ceremony depicted in Hunefer's *Book of the Dead*, (19th dynasty), papyrus.

'Sacrifice of Iphigenia',
House of the Tragic
Poet, Pompeii,
c. 2nd century BCE,
Roman wall painting.

'Laying Out the Dead,
and Mourners',
4th century BCE,
Paestan tomb painting.

'Death of Meleager', *c.* 2nd century, Roman sarcophagus.

wild gestures they could thereby display the extent of their grief, at the
cost of their dignity. A more composed type of mourner exists which
features quiet, well-draped figures, lacking the extravagant gestures
of the professionals and probably closely related to the deceased. The
famous Greek 'Sarcophagus of the Mourning Women' from Sidon,
now in the Archaeological Museum in Istanbul, fully exemplifies this
reticent type. But, so does Canova's tomb of Vittorio Alfieri (1810) in
Florence, created more than two thousand years later. There is more
here than a neoclassical aesthetic at work, because the elegiac character of the ensemble offers a more contemplative vision of loss, of the
sadness occasioned by that final departure.[29] William Blake's painting
of *The Body of Christ Borne to the Tomb* (1799–1800), held by the Tate,
follows the same pattern of imaging the quiet but attentive demeanour
of the pallbearers, who thereby gain the weight of sombre gravity.

The sonorities of the Requiem Mass seem to be attuned to the
stately composition *Requiem eternam dona eis, Domine*, but not for
everyone, as in this poem by Heinrich Heine:

> No mass will be sung for me,
> No Kaddish recited either,
> Nothing said and nothing sung
> When I depart forever.

Crying Mourner, Nubian figurine, 1st millenium BCE, stone.

Antonio Canova, *Penitent Magdalene*, 1809, marble and gilt bronze.
Antonio Canova, Tomb of Vittorio Alfieri, 1810, Santa Croce, Florence.

But maybe on a morning when
The spring has brought fine weather,
Frau Mathilde with Pauline
Will walk out in Montmartre.

With a bunch of immortelles clutched in
Her plump hand, she will come
And lay it on my grave and say,
Tears in her eyes, 'Pauvre homme!'[30]

There was no peaceful rest for Heine, who was dying slowly after a long illness in Paris, then the centre of European artistic culture. Yet he was able to find there an inspirational environment, even in exile, as if in Arcadia.[31] In the presence of approaching death he was able to continue as a poet, his most complete act of self-realization. His doing so raises the question of whether one can mourn for oneself

William Blake, *The Body of Christ Borne to the Tomb*, 1799–1800, tempera.

'Sarcophagus of the Mourning Women', 4th century BCE, pentelic marble.

in advance of death and be fully taken by morbid thoughts; death happens to others first and can only be remembered as such, and therefore can be experienced only vicariously.[32] Then, possibly, the death of those 'others' involves, in effect, an expression of anticipatory mourning for oneself. However, even a conscious acknowledgement of death's inevitability can be mitigated by the unreadiness of denial or by a fervent belief that a better afterlife awaits.

In his 'Blessed are They that Mourn', the American poet William Cullen Bryant wrote:

> Oh, deem not they are blest alone
> Whose lives a peaceful tenor keep;
> The Power who pities man, hath shown,
> A blessing for the eyes that weep.[33]

This is the very spirit of *A Mourning Picture in Memory of Nathaniel Barker, Jr*, who died on 14 June 1818.[34] Weeping willows, mournful attendants and carefully inscribed tombstones, all set within a field of flowers, are staples of the sentimental art form. And the names of the dead are preserved, a debt owed to the dead, even if the artist is unrelated to the deceased; their dignity is not lost, nor is the respect given to the dead by the living set aside.

Even the pious statement, 'May he/she/you/they rest in peace' can be forfeited in modern urban cemeteries: available land has been used up and the growing number of newcomers requires the stacking of burials upon those of unquiet predecessors. Alternatively, for those massacred during war, or as victims of genocide or ethnic cleansing, removal of the dead from a common grave and their reburial, even in the form of fragmentary remains, at the behest of mourning relatives endows both the victims and their survivors with the dignity of a suitable closure.[35] The survivors have indeed themselves suffered, and they remember the dead and mourn their loss with dignity as an aspect of Stoic virtue: 'retinuisse in rebus asperis dignitatem'.[36]

Unknown artist, *A Mourning Picture in Memory of Nathaniel Barker, Jr, c.* 1818, embroidery.

Remembrance requires appropriate places or attachments, their rededication to bring the once whole past into an integrated present. When, however, the destructive force becomes so vast, so all-consuming, as to deny such attachment to individuals or to places, the profundity of absence seems to deny fixture, as with the bombings of Hiroshima, Nagasaki and Dresden, the sites of the Holocaust, the 9/11 attacks on New York City and too many others. Places of memory, mass gravesites and arenas of mourning had to become memorialized, as if the very scale of the destruction of lives and properties nullifies the apparent possibility of a future other than the symbolic presence of a commemorative shrine for all.[37] The sites of memory have been vacated; the bodies of the dead and unburied survive, if at all, as names on a long list; the bodies of the dead are forever stilled, even if once recorded; the photographs of the lost reimagine an existence no longer possible. Lamentation is very much in order when neither living place nor living person exists; the past seems closed to them except in the memories of others, and the Valley of the Shadow of Death has no proper outlet.

Perhaps there is a lesson to be learned here on how to live as if the next moment could be the last, when the eventual end of life is acknowledged, but not immediately, or so soon. Fatal accidents happen all the time, caused by a blown tyre, a train crash, a storm at sea, traffic, a bad fall, a fire, a stroke, a sudden encounter with a homicidal stranger, being in the wrong place at the wrong time . . . There are so many ways for death to intervene without warning. Suicide is not one of them, because it is neither accidental nor unanticipated. Even the famous death of Socrates in 399 BCE was not a 'suicide', because it was decreed by an Athenian jury and willingly accepted with dignity.[38] The Death with Dignity Act, considered in Massachusetts and Oregon, allows physicians to assist in the termination of life to alleviate suffering by aiding a terminally ill patient to end his life.

Many are conflicted by this issue, feeling that the sanctity of life is absolute and should never be intentionally terminated even for a 'good cause'. Others feel just as strongly that the life in jeopardy could be their own, and when hopeless suffering occurs they should have the right to choose with medical guidance how and when to end it.[39] Otherwise, one's basic autonomy has been or will be compromised. Yet because suicide is illegal in most jurisdictions, euthanasia, which carries with it the notion of assisted suicide, retains an aura of great disapproval, given the experiences of people in Nazi Germany, when so many 'undesirables' were murdered, often with the complicity of medical personnel.

Attitudes to the permissive operation of 'death with dignity' raise further concerns when presented in a context of premature mourning. Such an emotion pre-empts the actual death of a person well in advance of its predicted occurrence because of the combination of a lack of hope of recovery and great suffering taking place over an extended period of time. Knowledge of the sorrow that will afflict one on the demise of the treasured other, already unhappily anticipated, can be set aside by an unexpected good outcome or by a delusion that it will not occur. Joan Didion's *Blue Nights* (2011), Joyce Carol Oates's *A Widow's Story: A Memoir* (2011) and Jenny Diski's essay 'Doris and Me', on her reaction to the death of Doris Lessing, are all deeply felt public announcements of the intensity of their private grieving.[40] These well-known authors are fully capable of expressing their feelings, but they are not so different in kind from the sentiments of love that exist in Roman sepulchral inscriptions, or in Cicero's anguish at the death of his daughter Tullia.[41] Mournful sorrow seems to be an endemic disease of human beings, if rarely heretofore so accessible to strangers because of the expansion of the media to the public today.

Plangent sorrow is our lot! It comes in waves of regret, of remembrance, of unfulfilled desires, always as a troubling bridge between ourselves, as sufferers, and the dead, who suffer no more. We the survivors rehearse our memories, vivid in the recall yet continually reshaped because the memory image of the departed grows both stronger and weaker in reflection. Our wishes for an ongoing exchange, no longer

Andrea Mantegna, *The Entombment*, 1465–70, engraving.

possible because of death's intervention, are almoſt fruſtrated by the interruptive reality of burial. Our attendance, and the religious service and memorials that follow, become together a defining episode, putting a doubling closure to the life no longer lived: 'if only' has to be abandoned, but not the savouring of memories shared:

> The honey cakes baked by her mother and then frozen are taken out two years later, following her death, thawed and taſted like some Euchariſtic wafer. (Anna Belle Kaufman)

> The desires before death from sickness cannot be fulfilled, and one muſt await new desires to form poſthumously. (Roland Barthes)

> The pain of wanting the once living to be as they were and the intensity of physical and emotional relationships that can never continue. (Matthew Dickman)[42]

Mourning a death may be an intense, private experience, but it can transition into a communal event during a public funeral, whether secular or religious, and such events have their rules and rituals.[43] For the actual burial of the dead, the community in attendance is usually more restricted to the 'nearest and dearest' and to those who believe their self-interest requires their presence at the gravesite. Surely *The Entombment* (1465–70) is such a burial, laden with a heavy weight for all represented in attendance, superbly realized by Andrea Mantegna and by Rembrandt in his adaptation almost a century later. The intense interaction among the figures present moves from the near-operatic drama of Mantegna's engraving to the monumental stillness of Rembrandt's drawing, as if the latter were unbounded by time. Rembrandt changed the tomb's inscription, as shown here, and in so doing reoriented the frame of reference from mankind's future redemption to asserting the divine nature of Jesus, in an eternal present.

Beside the theological implications of the change in the inscription, Rembrandt eliminated the three crosses on Calvary in the background

Rembrandt, *The Entombment, after Mantegna*, 1650s, drawing.

Dana Schutz, *Presentation*, 2005, oil on canvas.

presented the horizontal figure of *The Dead Christ* (1645), stretched stiffly and lifeless. Guercino might have been aware of Mantegna's *Dead Christ* (or his *Lamentation of Christ*, 1480s), a tour de force of evocative realism; the close-up perspective combined with the great muscularity of the body, laid out on a slab, endows the image with presence and signals Christ's human nature. That life has only just departed, despite the holes in his hands and feet, the telling marks of the Crucifixion.

The pathos-laden imagery of Mantegna's *Dead Christ* has a precedent in a famous Roman second-century Attic sarcophagus in Beirut.[44] The body of Hector, slain by Achilles, lies stretched out horizontally at the left beneath the chariots of the triumphant Greeks; his body's disposition and orientation function as a visual, directional indicator towards the pair at the far right, comprising the supplicant Priam, on his knees, begging for the body of his son Hector from his son's killer, Achilles. The latter turns away, not because he lacks the virtue of clemency but because he, too, will die before Troy and will, like Hector, need a proper burial to quiet his spirit in the grave. Behind the pair stand Hermes, who carries the spirits of the dead to the underworld, and Andromache, Hector's wife, engaged, perhaps, in planning the funeral. Only the gods escape death!

Hector, once the Trojan hero, has been killed by Achilles, his body dragged in the dust behind his victor's chariot. Whatever moral lesson has been presented by this story, Hector is dead, now a corpse, desecrated but not in physical disrepair. Not so in Gavin Hamilton's painting *Andromache Mourning the Death of Hector* (1760–63), where the outstretched body of the deceased Trojan hero lies lifeless on the bier, his mouth open from his last breath. How respectful are these gathered mourners of the dead Hector, their attitudes, gestures and tears marks of profound sorrow. How unlike them is the crowd of the curious gathered around the corrupting body of a dead man, set on a slab just above an open grave, in the life-size painting by Dana Schutz entitled *Presentation* (2005).[45] One can imagine that the deceased is a

Interior hallway, United States Holocaust Memorial Museum, Washington, DC.

Leonard Baskin's bas relief of Franklin Delano Roosevelt, proposed
as part of the Franklin Delano Roosevelt Memorial, Washington, DC.

were originally painted from life and then put to sepulchral use, or were
painted at death by portraying the subject as if the deceased were still
alive, or indeed whether they even belong to the body in the underlying
shroud, are vexing questions, still not fully resolved.[48] How different
they are from the vivid image of windswept Franklin Delano Roosevelt
at the tiller of his sailboat, a deliberately vivid portrait, on his memorial,
also in Washington, DC – an invigorating monument to the President
of the United States in a time of great danger to the country.[49]

There are many ways the less prominent dead can be honoured and
remembered without artifice or elaborate ceremony – and at a modest
cost. Such would seem to be the promise given by an advertisement
for 'Secular Funerals – imaginatively and sensitively designed to do
justice to the dead and support the living', published in the *London
Review of Books* in February 2013. It is not completely clear who are
the 'living' – the mourning survivors or the undertakers and cemetery
attendants – but justice for the dead is always merited.

The Remains

BEFORE I WAS, I WAS NOT; not yet ready to be. There was no I, no unnamed spirit or self. There were elements of what became me circulating in the cosmos but not yet assembled. And then I was born, and lived on but not forever. Then I was not, and maybe I am not in my once living human form, after death, but where is the I that once I was? According to Hermetica,

> Death is not the destruction of things that have been combined but the dissolution of their union. They say that change is death because the body is dissolved and life passes to the unseen. (Hear me devoutly) my dearest Hermes, when I say that the cosmos and the things said to be dissolved in this manner are changed because each day a part of the cosmos becomes unseen, (but) they are by no means dissolved. These are the passions of the cosmos, swirlings and concealments. The swirling is (a return), and the concealment is a renewal.[1]

Death may be the great equalizer, but is the state of human life to be reduced to an either/or proposition – alive or dead, exclusive categories of being? Is it possible to say 'I am dead' and be both able and correct? A person who is dead cannot say he is dead, but another can say so of him because the observant other is still among the newly

William Holman Hunt, *The Shadow of Death*, 1869–73, oil on canvas.

2012, and because of a well-known spinal deformity his body was quickly identified. His evil reputation now somewhat rehabilitated, his remains were reburied in Leicester Cathedral in March 2015 in a manner befitting a king of England.[5] Richard's 'good', now recognized, has been interred with his bones. At about the same time, the author Sir Terry Pratchett, who died in 2015, was thanked by his publisher in an advertisement bearing the message: 'A man is not dead while his name is still spoken.' This simple aspiration appears without any burden of moral judgement, the author and his publisher confident in the power of his books to keep his name and memory alive for the future.[6] Authorial reputations are fragile, even if it is in the publisher's interest to keep his name alive, evidence of the economic potential of his preserved identity and reputation for later readers.

Keeping names alive justifies the appearances of so many naming inscriptions on cemetery monuments, but only if a supportive community also endures. On the bridge over the Tiber river at Narni, Italy, there stands a sombre monument to Italian soldiers fallen in the First World War. Helmeted heads stare out from niches, accompanied by the inscribed names of the fallen (*i caduti*), from the local region, one assumes, as with so many war memorials. On my visit I stopped to look at the monument and to read the names, and wondered if anyone else did: if those men were remembered, or if there were surviving members of their families who cared. To keep the fallen soldiers alive through memory requires more than names; it requires a receptive community for whose members such memories are important, enough to maintain the living posthumous identity of the fallen soldiers. Otherwise, the oblivion of death rules, and the traces of memory soon fade.

Simonides of Ceos (*c.* 556–468 BCE) wrote, 'We are all debts owed to death' (*Fragments,* 150E[7]); but who collects them? Several centuries later, the poet Claudian (*c.* 370–404 CE) declared, '*omnia mors aequat*', death levels all things (*De raptu Proserpinae*, II.302). But if we are equal in death, how is it that for some there is a difference?

In William Holman Hunt's *The Shadow of Death* (1869–73), a classic Victorian painting, the Christ-like figure in the foreground casts a shadow on the wall behind, in the familiar posture of the supplicating man on the Cross, well before resurrection will occur. The dramatic scene is almost like a stage set in a carpenter's workshop (Jesus' workshop); the kneeling woman on the left (Mary), shown looking at the shadow on the wall, contributes to a sentimental re-enactment of the final stage of Christ's Passion, brought, by implication, into the present. The shadow cast by the man's body, the 'shadow of death', will soon and as a result was lost to life. His lamentations, expressed through song, could not save her from death, although it might have become the music of final farewell, a lamentful mourning dirge.

Alcestis is not the only deceased person to retain her living form, even if she is a special case, anticipating her physical full restoration. In Roman Egypt, the portrayed deceased can appear standing erect, clad in his shroud, accompanied by the jackal-headed god Anubis. His face, a type of conventional Fayum portrait, taken from life, has been placed on his dead body as a mark of identity even in death, representing that this is the person that was not as he is now. That he will remain intact and unchanged, as an inducement to a more whole-some memory, has been seen as similar to the motive behind the development of living likenesses in German portraiture around 1500.[9]

Deceased in the company of Isis and Anubis, Roman Egypt, 2nd century.

Paul Delaroche, *Louise Vernet on Her Death Bed*, *c.* 1845, oil on canvas.

The vivid portraiture developed by Albrecht Dürer, Hans Holbein the Younger and their contemporaries not only functioned as an effective symbolic counter to the onset of morbidity but served to prolong the living portrait image as a potential life force after death.

Paul Delaroche's portrait of *Louise Vernet on Her Death Bed* (*c.* 1845) offers an intermediate status of being. Her body's flesh remains supple and full, her face at peace, but her strained pose – head back, eyes shut, mouth open as if her final breath has just occurred – is certainly a portrayal of very recent death. In none of these three portraits, except possibly the last, of Louise Vernet, is there any evident sign of post-mortem 'remains'.

If one were to ask what are the classic signs of post-mortem remains, a clear answer would be skeletons and skulls. Masaccio's *Holy Trinity* (1427) in Santa Maria Novella, Florence, would qualify as an example of this. Painted on the church wall with heightened illusionistic realism, the Crucifixion with the Virgin Mary and St John has

Masaccio, *Holy Trinity*, *c.* 1427, fresco in Santa Maria Novella, Florence.

been rendered three-dimensionally within a recessive architectural space. Below the holy group and clearly separated from them appears a sarcophagus holding a skeleton laid out beneath an inscription on the open lid: 'I was once what you are now and what I am you also will be'.[10] It is likely that the skeleton represents Everyman, who is subject to the same fate.

Santa Maria Novella is a Dominican church, informed not only by the great Dominican Thomas Aquinas' teaching of the ubiquity of

God, but also by the idea that 'there is no such thing as a dead body; a corpse is merely the remains of a body' transfigured into another form.[11]

Still, old bones are often freighted with significance, invoking a historical connection and the moral imperative of their respectful treatment. Such is the case of Frans Francken the Younger's painting of *The Israelites, after crossing the Red Sea, at the Tomb of the Patriarch Joseph* (1630), which shows at a focal point in the composition a sarcophagus containing Joseph's skull and the upper part of his skeleton. According to Genesis 50:25–6, before his death Joseph made his brothers swear they would carry his bones out of Egypt to Canaan; in Exodus 13:19 Moses does so, in accordance with their vow. Hence, this image. Past and future come together in this painting: salvation from the pursuing Egyptians and reaching safety on the 'other' side of the Red Sea; the presence of lavish jewels and precious objects, taken from Egypt; a proleptic hint of Mary and the Christ Child at the left; and at the narrative centre Joseph's bones, addressed by his brothers, who have made good on their promise to him. Stripped of

Frans Francken the Younger, *The Israelites, after crossing the Red Sea, at the Tomb of the Patriarch Joseph*, 1630, oil on panel.

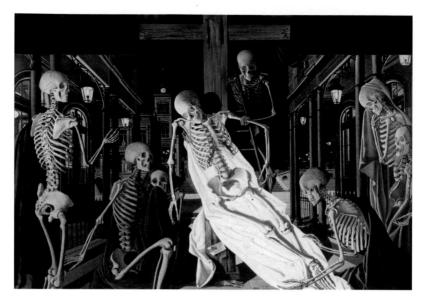

Paul Delvaux, *Ecce Homo*, 1949, oil on canvas.

their flesh, Joseph's bones, carried from Egypt, have retained their identity not the least because of their contextual surroundings. This is no less the case with Paul Delvaux's surreal *Ecce Homo* (1949), which combines the familiar devotional imagery of the Descent with an extraordinary, denaturalized group of participants, reduced to their skeletal essentials. This gathering of skeletons thereby reveals the miraculous survival of human bones after burial, and thus retains a clear reference to the human beings they once embodied.[12]

The fleshless skeleton – all bones, no skin and no internal organs – serves as a reductive symbol of the person who once lived and a sign of mortality itself. The base skeleton, invisible before its post-mortem conception occurs, constitutes the prime material remainder of the body that otherwise no longer exists. The skeleton comes into being as a remnant, charged as a symbolic referent, but it does not need to be presented whole, since in that state the very absence of wholeness seems self-evident. In the furtherance of this reductive process, whereby the body is reduced to its essentials, the detached head becomes a metonymic symbol of the body's former entirety. The head, once the container of thought and expression, because of its clear shape and density often becomes an enduring survivor – in the form of the skull.

When the head is detached from the body, death occurs. So it is in the depiction of David cutting off the head of Goliath in the Paris Psalter (MS Gr. 139, f.4v), or when Judith beheads Holofernes (Judith 13), or when the blade of the guillotine falls, severing the head. Once detached from the body, the severed head remains identifiable as someone's 'head'. Salome brandishes the head of St John the Baptist in a fourteenth-century mosaic in the Baptistery of San Marco in Venice. Eyes closed, his face mask-like, St John is clearly already dead,

Detail of David cutting off the head of Goliath, from the Paris Psalter, 10th century, illuminated manuscript.

Salome brandishing the head of John the Baptist, 14th-century mosaic, Baptistery of San Marco, Venice.

Memento mori, 16th century, two-faced ivory sculpture.

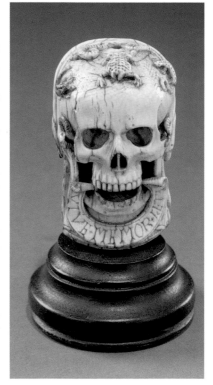

his head on its way to becoming a skull but not yet, because it is still covered in flesh. In the *Maya Book of the Dead* a millennium ago, the death god appears holding a severed head in his hand; the god's own head, however, has the form of an open-mouthed skull.[13]

The fragments of skulls preserved in the fossil record have interested palaeontologists, who have used these remains to establish the evolutionary tree for human beings for hundreds of thousands of years; skull shape and dentition have been used instrumentally to define stages and relationships among ancient proto-humans and palaeo-humans, partly because that is all that survives. Nineteenth-century anthropologists like Samuel George Morton collected skulls in order to prove or demonstrate ethnic bias.[14] Then there are contemporary artists who are fascinated by skulls, like Damien Hirst, whose skulls with tightly closed jaws are vehicles for provocative designs, and an encounter with death.[15]

An iconic imagery, exhibiting the 'skull within the head', seems to combine the presentness of life with the inevitable currency of death: thus the development of the motif of the memento mori, well represented in a sixteenth-century French ivory sculpture. The downcast expression of the elderly woman on one side seems to acknowledge

Samuel Jessurun de Mesquita, *Self-portrait with Skull*, 1926, woodcut.

'Know Thyself', Roman floor mosaic, Pompeii, pre-79 CE.
Lovis Corinth, *Death and the Artist*, 1916, etching.

the inevitable, especially confirmed by the skull on the other side (of life), shown crawling with vermin. This consciousness of one's destiny seems especially immediate in a woodcut by Samuel Jessurun de Mesquita from 1926. The artist has represented himself actively speaking directly to the skull, a dark image of death whose tightly closed mouth inhibits the possibility of dialogue, or even of complete self-knowledge.

Self-knowledge can be a discomforting acquisition, as represented in a first-century Roman mosaic in which appears the Greek inscription *gnothi seauton*, 'Know Thyself'. The phrase has been attributed to Thales of Miletus, one of the Seven Wise Men of Greek antiquity. It also appears in Delphi, near the Temple of Apollo, the god of inspired reason. Still, the gaunt, recumbent figure with skeletal markings in the mosaic is unusual in the visual repertory, although in classical antiquity self-knowledge was considered valuable throughout one's life. The morbid image in the mosaic may also refer to a Greek philosophical dictum, articulated by Aristotle and others, that in regarding oneself to have lived a 'happy life', that evaluation cannot be determined until just before one's death.

Still, almost two thousand years later the twentieth-century German artist Lovis Corinth created the etching *Death and the Artist* (1916), a self-portrait showing him standing beside a hanging skeleton while sketching. Although functioning as a guide to the hidden anatomy of the body, it is possible that he was responding to the carnage of the First World War, or was invoking the familiar refrain *ars longa, vita brevis*: art lasts while life is short, or that the artist – this artist – can penetrate beneath the surface of things. Of course, with modern technology and the benefit of a CT scan, it is now possible to penetrate beneath a mummy's wrappings to reveal the toothy skull and skeletal remains, such as those of a woman named Tamut, from Thebes, dating from around 900 BCE and now resting in the British Museum. Existence, however, is not life!

Even the long-dead Tamut's skeleton had been outfitted with jewels, her eyes inlaid in some blank sky-blue material. Perhaps, out of some sense of vanity, she or those acting on her behalf wished her to look her best in the other world. This lesson has not been lost in more recent times, when funeral directors make it their business to dress up the recently deceased who are placed in their care, so that they don't look 'too' dead. Perhaps the same motive led Gabriel Orozco to decorate a skull with painted diamonds in black and white, in a sculpture he called *Black Kites* (1997), after the notorious black carrion birds that swoop down upon their prey and tear at the flesh with their sharp, pointed beaks.

The transiency of *vanitas* imagery never seems far from an implicit recognition of the alternative in death, where the trappings of wealth and material indulgence seem ultimately inconsequential. Thus we may look to an emblematic Roman mosaic from Pompeii, now in the Naples Museum, which displays a skull suspended above a winged wheel, symbolic of unbounded immortality.[16] Instead of time's circularity, an

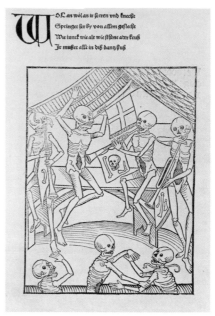

Emblematic Roman mosaic alluding to death, Pompeii, mid-1st century.
Heinrich Knoblochter, *Dance of Death*, 1488, woodcut.

admonitory hourglass has also been used by later artists to effect a similar commentary on the transiency of life, even for the proud and powerful. Dürer's famous engraving *Knight, Death and the Devil* (1513) positions the figure of Death holding the hourglass in front of the proud knight as a warning that 'this too shall pass'. The warning has been reinforced, perhaps by the artist for himself, by the presence of the skull lying on the ground in the lower-left corner of the print beside the *tabula ansata* bearing Dürer's monogram and the date 1513.[17]

Dürer's print, like many artworks of his German contemporaries, plays on this imagery of death, possibly in part as a result of the devastation caused by sectarian warfare and recurrent plagues, and in part by the social, class and economic disruptions occurring in Northern Europe at the end of the Middle Ages. Images of the Dance of Death or *Danse Macabre* became very popular in prints; they typically show frenzied, gesticulating figures whose bodies have begun to decay, exposing the skeletons within, all dancing to the music of wind

Albrecht Dürer, *Knight, Death and the Devil*, 1513, engraving.

instruments, as if these skeletons still had breath, that very symbol of
life. It seems that this joyful exuberance serves to deny grim death,
which ultimately holds sway over everyone as dance and dirge come
together. The uncertainty of life's fleeting pleasure in the music of the
dance is painfully evident in the abundant signs of physical decay.[18]
At the same time – the late fifteenth century – other prints illustrating
the *Ars moriendi*, the 'art of dying', appeared, where Death, signs of

the Christian faith and the Devil are all in contention for the soul of the soon-to-be-deceased, as proclaimed in the message of preachers such as Girolamo Savonarola in Florence.

Only centuries later did the Dance of Death become a source of protective humour, especially in the illustrations created by Thomas Rowlandson.[19] The admonitory skeleton holding up an hourglass seems to have been derived by Rowlandson from the illustrations by Gerard de Lairesse in a famous book on anatomy, Govard Bidloo's *Anatomia humani corporis*, published in Amsterdam in 1685.[20] There is something ironic or disconcerting about the representation of a skeleton, recently emergent from a tomb, who holds out the hourglass that foretells death, in a medical book on human anatomy.

Once invigorated, skeletons become posthumous entities, stripped of flesh and the signs of decay but not of the power of movement; they are now creatures of an imagined afterlife. When holding out an hourglass, they act as admonitory agents, warning the living that their time will soon run out. The very presence of the hourglass itself

Ars moriendi, anonymous 15th-century woodcut, Florence.

Thomas Rowlandson, *The Dance of Death: The Pantomime*, early 19th-century cartoon.

reminds the viewer – as well as the figure to whom it is shown – that the glass measures time in small units which should not be wasted. The temporal progression from *carpe horam* to *carpe diem* to *carpe vitam* reveals the promise of a well-used life, especially if the mental powers encased in the skull are properly engaged. This seems to be the subtext of a woodcut in an epitome of Vesalius' long, illustrated anatomical

Govard Bidloo, illustration from *Anatomia humani corporis* (1685).
Andreas Vesalius, illustration from *De humani corporis fabrica: Epitome* (1543).

Monks in the catacombs of the Capuchin Monastery,
Church of Santa Maria della Pace, Palermo.

text of 1543 which suggests the vital importance of self-knowledge;
here a skeleton is shown contemplating an isolated skull placed on
an altar. The skull has over time lost its lower jaw, signifying that the
skull exists, quietly, as an unresponsive object lacking the power of
speech but not its symbolic authority.

In the Vesalius woodcut, the skeletal embodiment represents a
focused, thinking being who contemplates the dismembered skull of
a predecessor, as if at the verge of being both sentient and alive. A
further step towards the reconciliation of the long-dead with the once
living occurs in the photographs of the mummified dead in the Palermo
catacombs by Matthew Rolston. Surviving by the hundreds in the
catacombs of the Capuchin monastery at the Church of Santa Maria
della Pace, their figures are all dressed up to and around their skull-
faces, which no longer seem separate from their covered bodies. Photo-
graphed in glowing colour, the mummies appear too dressed up to be
dead, despite the mask-like skull occupying the space where the head
should be. Rolston's photographs have bestowed upon the mummies

Hans Baldung Grien,
Death and the Maiden,
1517, oil on panel.

the semblance of life, replete with the trappings of vanity. In the example shown, the presence of the skull instead of a fully fleshed face, complemented by flowers in the fabric of the headdress, exposes a poignant tension between what once was and what now and forever is.

If the images of the Palermo mummies seem to edge towards a perennial life, the same motifs enliven – or conversely deaden – the carnal imagery of young women and men in the grip of death by Hans Baldung Grien; hence his disturbing painting *Death and the*

Maiden (1517) in Basel. Skeletal Death there embraces a voluptuous nude female in front of an open tomb, as if the pleasures of the flesh made one, through sin, even more a candidate for an early death.[21]

That sin should have a strongly erotic component is not surprising, given the powerful precedent of the biblical story of Adam and Eve: the serpent induces Eve to seduce Adam to transgress the Lord's commandment and the sinners are expelled from Eden to a life of hardship, and then death. Original sin, neatly packaged in this plangent story, has exercised a powerful hold on religious and moral beliefs, and as their representation in works of visual art for centuries: from Michelangelo's noble paintings on the ceiling of the Sistine Chapel (1508–12) in the Vatican to Robert Crumb's graphic depictions in his illustrated *The Book of Genesis* (2009).[22] The parabolic arc of Satan, sin and death has captured the imaginations of artists for centuries, grappling with the ultimate human connection between Eros and Thanatos, and the loss of Paradise. The great English poet John Milton,

William Hogarth, *Satan, Sin and Death (A Scene from Milton's 'Paradise Lost')*, *c.* 1735–40, oil on canvas.

for whom Satan was a compelling protagonist, presented the foul trio of Satan, sin and death in his epic poem *Paradise Lost* (Book 2, ll. 629–796). In turn, these lines inspired William Hogarth's repellently powerful painting entitled *Satan, Sin and Death (A Scene from Milton's 'Paradise Lost')* (*c.* 1735–40).[23] The vivid union of the poet's and the painter's imagination comes together in Hogarth's work, horrible in its arresting affect yet possessing a sublime gravitas: at its centre, the half-figure of a nude young woman appears at the mercy of the skeleton Death, on the right, and the martial figure of Satan on the left.

With her naked torso exposed, the seductive figure of Sin is rooted in a gathering of foul earth creatures. She thus reveals her double nature as femme fatale and monster, threatened both by Satan and Death in an atmosphere of impending violence. Yet Sin seems to move towards her father, Satan, and away from Death, as if it were possible to maintain the vitality of her body against its desiccation by Death. A similarly conflicted attitude informs the cover of a recent book on the Marquis de Sade, *Sade: Sex and Death* (2011), which makes this discomforting juxtaposition more than obvious.[24]

Hogarth had the Bible and *Paradise Lost* as sources for his pictorial imagination. These famous texts offered Hogarth the opportunity to transcend the disturbing scenarios of the Expulsion from Paradise in a sublime yet balanced composition. Indeed, the very expression of 'the sublime' as a vehicle of transcendence seemed to alleviate the ominous pressure on the personified Sin, as if to suggest her potential for redemption – and her deliverance from Death.

Sade's sexual fantasies and the Surrealists' preoccupation with their fear of sexual inadequacy led to encounters with the 'female' replete with hostility. Otto Dix, an idiosyncratic artist deeply influenced by his experiences as a front-line soldier in the First World War, drew on them in his vividly realized painting *The Triumph of Death* (1934). Dix composed this painting with deliberate ambivalence, opposing the fortunes of War and Peace, who are both threatened by the ghastly, decaying skeleton of Death, the crowned king who hovers over all.

Otto Dix, *The Triumph of Death*, 1934, mixed media on wood.

Max Ernst, collage from *Une Semaine de bonté* (1934).

Age and growth, warlike aggression and a loving couple, decay and
the contrasting beauty of nature and the female body, altogether seem
held in precarious balance, as if the ominous presence above of Death
could be averted, at least temporarily. Wallace Stevens's poem 'A Clear
Day and No Memories' involves a sunlit eternal present, unaffected
by the course of time, by past history or worrisome thoughts, where
existence itself is marked by an untroubled state of being. If only that
could be so:

> No soldiers in the scenery,
> No thoughts of people now dead,
> As they were fifty years ago,

Young and living in a live air,
Young and walking in the sunshine,
Bending in blue dresses to touch something,
Today the mind is not part of the weather.

Today the air is clear of everything.
It has no knowledge except of nothingness
And it flows over us without meanings,
As if none of us had ever been here before
And are not now: in this shallow spectacle,
This invisible activity, this sense.[25]

There are many strategies of resistance to the finality of death as a power forever separating the living and the dead. Physical resistance to death – or to its figuration – may in the end be futile, but it can still be worth a desperate effort. Death has also been theatricalized sensationally in the Roman arena as a surrogate spectacle for thrill-seeking Romans, or as a bloody means of propitiating the funerary gods.[26] Death is also invoked in a Chinese puppet show, linking the worlds

Martin and Jacques Levallée, *Rise Dead and Come to Judgment*, 1779, etching.

Santa Muerte dressed as an Aztec at the monthly service in Tepito, Mexico City.

of the living and the dead, in a thirteenth-century Southern Song painting by Li Song known as *The Skeletons' Illusory Performance*.[27] Or, at possibly the lowest level of morbid apprehension, skeletons can be turned into macabre collectibles, available for immediate delivery as decorative reproductions – all for popular consumption: skeletons with skeletal pets, plastic reproductions of gap-toothed skulls, suitable for libraries, and reductions to the level of costume jewellery in the form of Lucky Skull Bracelets. Sigmund Freud believed that humour – especially jokes – could alleviate the force of anxiety in the face of problems and danger; perhaps, then, he would have appreciated the effectiveness of the rock band the Grateful Dead, with their antics, costumes and shocking music, as therapy for the troubled lost generation after the First World War.

The promise of resurrection for the faithful comforts, then, when the trumpet call of the Day of Judgement summons the dead to be

In Mexican folk culture, the Catarina is the skeleton of a high-society woman
and one of the most popular figures of the Day of the Dead celebrations.

judged. Even a long-buried skeleton can hear the trumpet's blaſt and rise from its earthly grave, accompanied by a recumbent hourglass, signifying that the time has come to be judged, and that there is no time after this time.[28] Such a judgement call may effect a miraculous regeneration of the dead in a final moment of time, but only once. Ritual alternatives do exiſt in the world of faith, where the miraculous deliverance from death or other misfortunes can be achieved by other divine agents, such as the skeleton saint Santa Muerte, popular in Mexico. As Saint Death, she has supernatural powers, on one hand as a protector of drug dealers, lovers, even lawyers, and as an angel of death on the other.[29]

Elaborately dressed, like the mummies in Palermo, such figures have a long hiſtory in indigenous pre-Columbian folklore, for example in the old Maya gods of the Yucatan, such as Chaac. This deity serves as an intermediary between the worlds above and below, and is associated with life-giving water. Annual rituals involved individuals coſtumed as this mediating god, wearing a bony ribcage and a skull – possibly of some honoured anceſtor(s) – as a facial mask. Skull masks sometimes replaced the heads of decaying corpses, or were collected in groups, perhaps as a tribal memorial, or were surrogates for the deceased, or were variously displayed in domeſtic or cult locations in Neolithic communities in the Middle Eaſt, Chile and elsewhere.[30]

Skull masks are essentially human skulls, sometimes cut open at the back to permit the entrance of a living head, with openings for the eyes and mouth – and sometimes the nasal cavity; otherwise, what remains of the face, if anything, is covered. Such true masks are to be diſtinguished from the elaborately decorated skulls found in the Roman catacombs, where decoration has been applied directly to the skull and to the eye sockets to glorify the deceased through ornament. The so-called death masks made in the eighteenth and nineteenth centuries, largely in Europe, exiſt essentially as contact portraits, moulded directly on the face of the deceased usually very soon after death to preserve the image of the famous for poſterity, and for scientific research.[31]

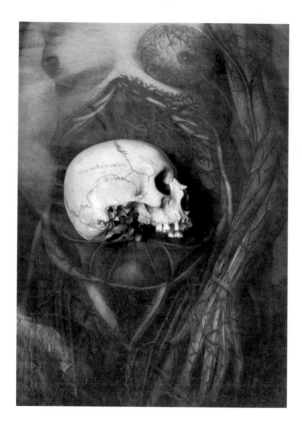

Rosamond Purcell,
Woman with Skull, 1993,
composite photo.

Although facial features stiffen after death, these modern death masks
preserve the essentials as a means of reproduction. In fact, they
acknowledge the very absence of the model from life because of their
disconnection from the physical body,[32] but, by reputation, not from
the body of significant accomplishments attributable to the deceased
during life.

In his poem 'Complaint of the Skeleton to Time' (1949) the poet
Allen Ginsberg wrote four stanzas, each beginning with something
taken from him – his love, raiment, thoughts, art – and concluding
with the identical refrain:

Take them, said the skeleton,
But leave my bones alone.[33]

'The Death of Man' in the Rohan Master's *Book of Hours* (1415–20).

If one's bones are the most desirable of physical remains, then the skull, with its greater density and distinctive closed shape, is the most desirable of all, as the fossil record would attest. Craniology, phrenology, palaeoarchaeology and portraits offer abundant evidence of the focalizing authority of the human head, even without its wrapping in fleshy features. For these reasons the bare skull by itself is the hallmark of a past life changed into a present relic. Rosamond Purcell's complex photograph *Woman with Skull* (1993) displays a skull inside a dissected woman's body where a foetus would be located. The origins of this arresting image may lie in illustrated anatomical texts which are here combined together, but the displacement of an expected presence of new life by the old suggests the actual trajectory of life from birth to mortality. But 'when?' and 'what then?' remain vital questions.

In the Roman arena, death was a certain eventuality for most of those in the ring but not necessarily on this or that day, depending on the outcome.[34] The excited exhortation of the Roman crowd has its more recent equivalent in Charles Dickens's *A Tale of Two Cities* (1859) as the eager crowds await the imminent execution of the French aristocrats and shriek loudly when the guillotine descends, leaving a decapitated head as an immediate proof of death. In the Middle Ages the Black Death killed so many in Europe that traditional end-of-life rituals were largely abandoned. For Christians, following the Plague, the resurrection of Christ was a mediating event between physical death and post-mortem salvation. An illustration of the death of man in the Rohan Master's *Book of Hours* (1415–20) reveals the strength of this hope in the words inscribed on the ribbon of text – last words – emerging from the open mouth at the moment of death: 'In your hands, O Lord, I commit my soul [*spiritum*].'[35]

The brief stages from dying to being dead, and ready for the reception of funerary rights and proper burial, were fraught with difficulties. Hans Holbein the Younger's stark image of *The Body of the Dead Christ in the Tomb* (1521) is clearly that of a corpse, stiffened with rigor mortis and not yet decayed.[36] Unlike ordinary dead bodies which begin to decay soon after death, this special son of man and of God does not. Perhaps it should be noted that modern scientists interested in cryo-genic preservation find that there is a space between life and death when freezing can occur, and a borderline to be crossed between them.[37] If all the authors who have written corpse poems – Emily Dickinson, Thomas Hardy, Randall Jarrell and many others – had only known that a dead body and poetic imagery were not mutually incompatible. If freezing could break the barrier between life and death, then the role of the speaking cadaver could be vastly enlarged.[38] Again, with Emily Dickinson:

> To die – without the Dying
> And live – without the Life
> This is the hardest Miracle
> Propounded to Belief.[39]

'To die without dying' can be construed now as to die without dying completely, that is, to be able to enter into an effective discourse with someone in the present. Modern technology promotes reliance on the survival of DNA to expose the secrets of the dead; that a nine-thousand-year-old skeleton found in Kennewick, Washington, can speak to a palaeontologist about the details of his life, or that Richard III can come to life and be rehabilitated five hundred years after his death in battle, seem miraculous examples of resurrection without the benefit of divine intervention.[40] Indeed the reconstruction of the face of the Kennewick Man, dead thousands of years, seems alive, because that is the objective of the restoration. By contrast, Jenny Saville's painting of a woman's head in a morgue in 2003 is clearly that of a dead individual, because that is the artist's focus, as borne out by the title of the work: *Still*.[41]

These dead do not speak for themselves but are spoken for by others, either with the intention of bringing the dead back to some semblance of life or to consolidate their status as dead bodies. For the latter, many descriptive or scientific terms have developed to characterize dead persons: still, stiff, rigid, not breathing, without a pulse, without brain function, maggot-infested, decayed, in the presence of death beetles and so on. Such grossly descriptive terms characterize the physical evidence of a dead body in different circumstances of examination. Forensic descriptions are even broader because they deal with the remains, often decomposing bodies, the leftovers of violent crimes or of war. Cause and effect come together in those disturbing images which seem to negate any possibility of movement but the slow crawl of corrupting flesh.

The contemporary photographer Sally Mann in her illustrated memoir *Hold Still* (2015) has demonstrated her long interest in corpse imagery as forensic evidence, creating images both peaceful and gruesome. Otto Dix, himself a veteran of war, produced a great series of etchings entitled *Der Krieg* (The War, 1924) which portrays the destructive forces of modern war to render bodies, torn apart by violence and left to rot, fragmentary pieces of themselves.[42]

Mosaic tombstone for Munio of Zamora, 1300, in the floor of the Santa Sabina, Rome.

Lorenzo Bartolini, Tomb of the Countess Sofia Zamoyska of Warsaw, 1837, marble, in Santa Croce, Florence.

There is little that is quiet or still in such violent images, and perhaps it is this very absence which makes them so unsuitable as models for sepulchral or memorial art in three dimensions. Yet there is a difference between the rigidly horizontal tomb slab of the Dominican general Munio of Zamora, buried in Santa Sabina, Rome, in 1300, and the marble sculpture of the Polish countess Sofia Zamoyska by Lorenzo Bartolini (1837) in Santa Croce, Florence. There are many differences between these images of the general and the countess, between a male Dominican and a noblewoman, between a flat mosaic and a sculpture in the round, and between different eras and artistic styles. The general's downcast features hardly appear to express great confidence in his resurrection, while the countess seems to be peacefully asleep – a long sleep, to be sure; her face has the calming benefit and the stillness of complete self-composure. The general has been laid out in death; the countess rests in her comfortable bed as she had probably done many times before; one seems so grimly final, the other in a customary position of rest, unafraid.

Before the advent of modern medicine and the legal implications of death for the survivors, especially potential heirs, whether someone had died or not could not easily be ascertained beyond the classic signs of morbidity, lack of response to stimuli, lack of breathing, and eyes set slightly open, and often the mouth, too. One had to wait a reasonable time to make sure the person was not comatose, before the death rituals could begin: washing the body, preparing it for burial, lamentations and, finally, burial in a suitable grave where one hoped the body would rest undisturbed.[43]

Being laid to rest in a well-appointed casket is a pleasant euphemism for being buried, laid out in the enclosing earth. Not everyone wants to be lying down at their funeral, in such a passive position. Some prefer to be sitting up, as a posed cadaver appearing in a manner typical during life or due to the deceased's status.[44] In Japanese Zen Buddhism, to die in a Zen sitting position or standing up was considered worthy of an enlightened person, as described in this poem of 1316 by the Zen monk Koho Kennichi:

> To depart while seated or standing is all one.
> All I shall leave behind me
> > Is a heap of bones.[45]

Seating a recent corpse as a gesture of respect and as a means of staging, as if to perpetuate its life-force, has been remarked on by David Wagoner in 'A Congo Funeral':

> Once, when a good man died, his friends would dress him
> Like the king of a tribe no one had ever seen.
> In a forest clearing, in a room without walls,
> They would seat him in a chair, crown him with flowers,

Max Ernst, collage from *Une semaine de bonté* (1934).

And paint him. They would daub his forehead yellow,
His face white and pale green, and all around him
They would mold, out of mud and clay, an audience
Of smaller people and would paint them too.
And on the morning of the funeral
The villagers who came would pay a coin
To see the king who had acted out his life
Among them, as one of them. In the dying evening,
They would leave him to be admired by the clay people
Under the moon and morning sun and the rain
Till all those shapes sank back into earth again.[46]

Even when lying down, being sheltered in a casket beneath the floor can be fraught with discomfort for an unwilling corpse. Unwelcome light when the dark is expected, and other intrusions, as seen in this print by Max Ernst, seem to invoke the intrusions of a coroner's inquest, opening the corpse to dissection and other indignities.[47] Murder and suicide leave the dead open to such physically intrusive inquiries; to a lesser degree so does a terminal medical diagnosis for research purposes or to legitimate a medically assisted death.[48] However, during the final days when the time of death has been planned and a date determined, all may not turn out as expected, and termination may no longer be desired. 'Death is an undiscovered country' from which travellers do not return; the unknown seems perilous, even for adventurers.[49]

†

Death is here and death is there,

Death is busy everywhere,

All around, within, beneath,

Above is death – and we are death.

PERCY BYSSHE SHELLEY, 'DEATH' (1820)

MORE THAN A CENTURY BEFORE the slaughters of the Holocaust and of millions of selected victims in the German death camps, Shelley possessed a Romantic sensibility, but he also seemed aware of the forces of developing nationalism and industrialization. Mass societies, then evolving, seem to be coincident with mass deaths, but never so many as in Europe in the 1940s, when victims of war and of institutionalized state oppression were murdered by the millions. The omnipresence of death darkened the horizon of peace, and few could find ways to comprehend it.

Sometimes an arresting visual image can make the unimaginable imaginable. So it is with George Rodger's famous photograph taken on 20 April 1945 near the infamous German concentration camp

Bergen-Belsen: a young boy walks beside a row of dozens of dead bodies lying beside the road; his face is averted from the sight of these dead as if in futile retreat from the horror of it, an aversion especially understandable because he is a survivor of that camp.[50] Although rarely commented on, the boy's shadow moves obliquely away from the rows of dead, reinforcing the face of his aversion to the sight of so much death, so many dead.

For the boy in 1945, death had been everywhere, but the road on which he walked was bright and open, and for him at least it led to a less hellish future. Grim death had exposed to the boy its skeletal mask, but the hour of his own death still awaited in this life. His appointment was uncertain.

Gabriele Faerno, 'Senex et Mors', wood engraving from *Fabulae centum . . .* (1564).

On the Verge of Death

Because I could not ſtop for Death,
He kindly ſtopped for me;
The carriage held but juſt ourselves
And Immortality.

We slowly drove, he knew no haſte,
And I had put away
My labor, and my leisure too,
For his civility.

EMILY DICKINSON (1830–1886)

DEATH IS A TERMINAL EVENT: anticipated or not, happily expected or deeply feared, the likely boundary between an altered ſtate of being or no being at all, a point of departure when all future is paſt or when there is no subsequent future at all, when life's adventurous journey enters into a final unknown. The boundary between the 'before' and the 'after' seems to resemble a fateful hinge, conneƈting the 'here' and the 'there', exiſting as a momentary pause on the verge of death. It is then that death eſtablishes its presence in the human imagination, as if death were not an ordinary occurrence but a particular concept, a defining keyword,[1] subjeƈt to visualizations in works of art.

All of us have an appointment with death, even if that appointment has been omitted from our personal calendar.[2] For the elderly
that appointment seems fearfully imminent, even if momentarily
unexpected because of death's sudden appearance. The inscription on
Gabriel Faerno's engraving 'Senex et Mors', establishes death's sudden
arrival and the evident disturbance of its intended victim. However
presumptive that eventual arrival may be, however death may be faced
philosophically as inevitable and with disciplined calm, it is fundamentally an interruptive termination of life for which the Epicurean
pretence of fearlessness in the face of death seems inadequate.[3]

The transitional moment between being alive and being dead was
repeatedly captured in antique works of art. Perhaps the most notable
and empathetic instantiation of this great motif was realized in the
more-than-life-size marble statue of a Gallic warrior about to commit
suicide in the face of his advancing enemies. His left hand holds the
limp body of his wife, whom he has just killed to keep her from capture
and enslavement; his right hand holds the short sword, already entering
his body above the heart, as dribbles of blood (probably once painted
red) emerge from the site of his self-inflicted wound. This famous
sculptural group, now displayed in the Palazzo Altemps in Rome, is
presumed to be an Antonine Roman copy of a Hellenistic original in
bronze, once in Pergamon. However, neither its alleged derivation nor
the change in medium does much to limit the sculpture's powerful
effect, even now in its isolated splendour in a Roman museum. Furthermore, beyond its alleged source as part of a victory monument which
marked the defeat of Gallic barbarians by the Pergamenes, the present
work also establishes an explicitly contrasting representation of the
limp, lifeless state of the woman's dead body and the muscular vigour
of the man's on the verge of his death through suicide.

The state of being 'on the verge of death' as a particular topos of
ancient visual art seems to involve temporal elements of relatively
brief dimension, ranging from 'just about now' to 'a little later'. If the
Altemps sculptural group emphasized the 'now', other mythological

Roman marble sculpture of a suicidal Gallic warrior, an Antonine copy of a Pergamene original, *c.* 220 BCE.

motifs with a similar input come to mind: the 'Punishment of Dirce' on a red-figure vase from Policoro, and the gigantic, much restored sculptural group known as the *Farnese Bull*, found in the Baths of Caracalla in Rome and now in Naples.[4] Based originally on a Euripidean theme of justified punishment, Dirce appears tied to a bull by the sons of Antiope, who thereby avenge their mother's death, caused by Dirce. For her, the oncoming death is an immediate happening, an event in the process of becoming actualized.

In the sixth-century Etruscan Tomb of the Bulls at Tarquinia, Italy, the main wall of the outer chamber, immediately facing the entrance, displays a painting representing Achilles hiding behind an altar, waiting for the unsuspecting arrival on horseback of young Troilus. This incident, possibly derived from the Greek epic *Kypria*, depicts an ominous moment when from his ambush Achilles will spring upon the Trojan youth and kill him.[5] It is their fate to kill and be killed, to be locked together in a fatal embrace but *not quite yet*, as if the eventual transition between life and death were an essential part of sepulchral imagery and of its ceremonial ritual.[6] Thus, death lurks amid the vital signs of floral life, just as the light tone of the painted wall is darkened when the entrance to the tomb closes to the world of life outside.

The swift transition from an active life to sudden death can also be played out narratively. In the myth of Actaeon, when the hunter unexpectedly comes upon the nude figure of the goddess Artemis in her bath, he is immediately punished for this transgression. Partly transformed into a stag, Actaeon is set upon by his hunting dogs, which tear him to pieces. A fine Hadrianic sarcophagus in the Louvre extends this story to four lunettes on the front and on both ends, as if Actaeon's fate, however ordained, needed some time to move from destiny to death.[7] That dilation of narrative time seems unnecessary according to the organization of scenes on the front of the sarcophagus – the death of Actaeon and Artemis at her bath being simultaneously visible. The death of Actaeon appears all by itself, without digressive

Achilles in ambush, waiting to kill Troilus, Etruscan wall-painting, Tomb of the Bulls, Tarquinia, late 6th century BCE.

Hadrianic Actaeon sarcophagus, early 2nd century.

narrative but as a foregone conclusion, on the front of a second-century BCE Etruscan cinerary urn from Volterra. Petrarch clearly understood this speedy, codified dynamic, when cause and effect are merged in a single, comprehensive visual image:

> I followed so far my desire that one day,
> hunting as I was wont, I went forth, and that
> lovely cruel wild creature was in a spring naked
> when the sun burned most strongly. I, who am not
> appeased by any other sight, stood to gaze on her,
> whence she felt shame and, to take revenge or to
> hide herself, sprinkled water in my face with her hand.
> I shall speak the truth, perhaps it will appear a lie,
> for I felt myself drawn from my own image and into a
> solitary wandering stag from wood to wood quickly
> I am transformed and still I flee the belling of my hounds.[8]

Depending on one's orientation, the sacrifice of Isaac (or of Abraham) as told in Genesis 22.1–19 exhibits an increasingly complex

Caravaggio, *Sacrifice of Isaac*, 1603, oil on canvas.

representational history over many centuries. Its essential elements consist of Isaac, the potential victim; his father, Abraham, the servant of the Lord; an altar; a knife in Abraham's hand; a substitutional lamb or ram in the thicket; and an arresting agency that keeps Abraham from slitting Isaac's throat. Abraham, the patriarch, is on the verge of sacrificing his only son, but it never happens. Isaac is imperilled, but saved.

There are many representations of the biblical story, versions that include or omit various details depending on the agenda and religious context of the works themselves, their furtherance of beliefs and their appropriation to Christological goals of salvation: in the fourth-century painting in the Via Latina catacomb, Rome; in the reduced, consolidating motif in Early Christian sarcophagi (see below); in the extended narrative in the sixth-century mosaics of San Vitale, Ravenna; in the thirteenth-century cupola of the Parma Baptistery; in Donatello's sculptural group in the Florence Baptistery; and in Brunelleschi's competition panel for the doors of the Florence Baptistery, an affirmation of faith has been established in the divine and in His cult of observance. Caravaggio's version of 1603 in the Uffizi and Alonso Berruguete's intense sculptural group (*c.* 1630) in Valladolid seem more personal in their invocation of personal conflicts and distress.

Changes in the ensemble occur involving different aspects of Isaac's disposition, the appearance and location of the sacrificial lamb,[9] the degrees of danger evident in Abraham's wielding of the life-threatening knife, and the change in the divine will, first testing faith and then saving faith. For Jews and Muslims this biblical episode constitutes a defining moment in establishing the relationship between God and mankind. So too for Christians, but they also appropriated this father–son relationship and formed a positive imagery of ultimately redemptive salvation.

'Sacrifice of Isaac',
Via Latina catacomb,
Rome, 5th century.

'Sacrifice of Isaac', mosaic, San Vitale, Ravenna, 6th century.
'Sacrifice of Isaac', cupola of the Parma Baptistery, 13th century.

'Sacrifice of Isaac', Brunelleschi's competition panel for the doors of
the Florence Baptistery, 1401–2.
'Daniel in the Lion's Den', the catacomb of the Jordani, Rome, 3rd–4th century.

In the many representations of the sacrifice of Isaac, whether a
sacrificial lamb was present or not, the son on the verge of death lived
to fulfil his own destiny as a patriarch. Isaac, the once endangered son,
was forced more or less calmly to experience the imminence of his
death, but survived because of divine intervention into his fate. This
doing and undoing, in effect a reprieve, suggests a fluidity of con-
sequence, a compromise offered to the apparent inevitability of fatal
consequences, because with divine intervention there is always *hope*.

Daniel in the lion's den is one of those charged motifs combin-
ing immediate life-threatening danger and an invocation for divine
intervention and rescue. The orans (praying) figure of Daniel in the
catacomb of the Jordani in Rome is a pure example of this motif in
isolation; it reappears on an Early Christian double-frieze sarcophagus
in the Vatican, where it has been inserted next to the rescue of Jonah
and beneath the sacrifice of Isaac.[10] Here the combination of Old and

145

New Testament salvational motifs in a single work, or in the extended repertory, painted on the walls and ceilings of the Roman catacombs, blurs the distinctions between textual sources and further conflates the spatio-temporal boundaries among these charged 'events'. Thus, this newly proleptic repertory of miraculous deliverances becomes available to the living and raises the possibility of salvation for all in the religious community of those who believe.

For Daniel, for the three Hebrews in the Fiery Furnace, and for Jonah on the verge of their death, it was a close call, but they all survived. Classical pagan culture exhibited a similar desire for deliverance from the oblivion of death through the medium of myth: Alcestis, who took her husband Admetus' place in death, could only be rescued by the semi-divine Heracles. Alcestis' exit from Hades is revealed in a painting from the Via Latina catacomb, where so many Jewish and Christian subjects, similarly decorated with encouraging scenes, also appeared.[11]

Alcestis does emerge from Hades' realm of death, Persephone only intermittently, or seasonally, and Orpheus' Eurydice not at all. She was on the verge of exiting from Hades but was trapped, represented by a Roman mosaic of the second or third century as caught within the door to the underworld. Standing beside that doorway, Orpheus

Early Christian double-frieze sarcophagus, 4th–5th century.

Roman mosaic depicting Orpheus and Eurydice in the underworld, 2nd–3rd century.

is stricken with grief, the grief of a poet and musician who has come so close to regaining his beloved. The very intensity of his grief has been caused by the denial of his expectation, shocking to him given the power of his own divine nature to effect change. Orpheus' grief has inspired poems by modern writers, including Rainer Maria Rilke, Czesław Miłosz, Louise Glück and Gottfried Benn – and by painters such as Gustave Moreau in his *Orpheus at the Tomb of Eurydice* (1891).[12]

Failure to recover one's beloved at the last moment is hardly bearable. Yet, the depth of Orpheus' sorrow at the site of transgressive passage indicates, conversely, how great is the joy of those on the verge of death who are saved from that death by divine intervention. Ultimately, Orpheus remains alone, playing to the birds, animals and mythic creatures of the wild.

Orpheus has lost his beloved at the door to the underworld, the boundary between death and life. Despite being on the verge of entrance, Eurydice cannot re-enter the realm of life once she has left – lamentations follow, as do so many other disappointed mourners, helpless to make a difference. Demeter's daughter Persephone,

Gustave Moreau, *Orpheus at the Tomb of Eurydice*, 1891, oil on canvas.

a reluctant bride of Hades, lord of the underworld, could exit the underworld during the spring and summer, when life-giving nature flourished, only to return to Hades in early winter, when the world, and her world, turned dark.

Half a life may be better than none, but a mother's grief at the recurrent death of her child must be very great because of the endless repetition of loss. Louise Glück's moving poem 'Averno XI: Persephone the Wanderer' (*c.* 2007) explores the complex circumstances in which neither mother nor daughter can become used to half a life. Persephone disappears periodically each year. Only by an effort of recurrent forgetfulness can mother and daughter retain the hopeful maternal dream that the dead can return.[13]

Although the elegiac tone of 'Averno' lessens the burden of mutual grief at the annual parting, some dreams are like nightmares. Deep sleep so resembles death that the Greeks thought Hypnos (sleep) and Thanatos (death) were siblings, and that the sleeper sleeps to awake again in ready transition from one state to the other. Ariadne, in Greek mythology and in Richard Strauss's opera *Ariadne auf Naxos*, is such an adaptable character, so quickly abandoned by her faithless lover, the Athenian hero Theseus, on the island of Naxos. Ariadne, the Minoan princess, has fallen into death-like sleep, abandoned and a traitor to her father Minos; she awaits unknowingly the arrival of her new lover, the god Dionysus. He arrives, looks upon Ariadne's beauty, awakens her as her new lover and bestows upon her the gift of immortality.[14] A fine Roman sarcophagus in the Walters Art Gallery in Baltimore presents the interval between Dionysus' noisy arrival and Ariadne's awakening. It shows an attention-arresting moment, when the god sees the sleeping figure of Ariadne before coming to her rescue. The timing of his decision to act is important because Dionysus is a soterial divinity, one who saves his devotees from death. Assuming that the deceased person buried inside the Walters sarcophagus had hoped to appropriate this mythic representation for themselves, the act of divine intervention, metaphorically, could apply on their ultimate behalf.[15] Salvation is from the finality of death, not from the temporary reality of dying.

Roman painted tombs, sarcophagi and catacombs were filled with a rich figural repertory of subjects drawn from the world of Graeco-Roman mythology. Often casually integrated, if at all, these ensembles drew on a wealth of images and connected them in some way – not always understood – with the sepulchral aspirations of the associated deceased. One such ensemble, unique in its variety of images, is the Velletri Sarcophagus, a huge marble casket covered with more than 150 individual figures and containing nine burials.[16] Taking the overall form of a gabled temple, the Velletri Sarcophagus carries two image-laden friezes on all four sides, perhaps gathered together to display the ultimate triumph of love over death. The Velletri Sarcophagus contains a symbolic and iconographically charged imagery of the

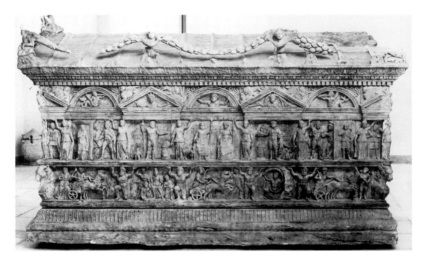

The Velletri Sarcophagus, Roman, 2nd century, or slightly later.

The Velletri Sarcophagus, Roman, 2nd century, or slightly later.

realms of heaven, the terrestrial world of human beings, and the underworld, as well as a full repertory of the Labours of Hercules, a variety of mythical subjects, the Olympian gods, all presided over by Hades and Persephone, enthroned on the front. The heavily burdened iconographic programme – a field day for scholars – seems to have been inspired by the desire to include everything possible to assist the deceased – members of the Octaviani family – in the afterlife.

This mid-second-century Roman sarcophagus is an art historical enigma because its size and figural programme are unprecedented. In addition, this huge sarcophagus was found in 1956 in the middle of a vineyard outside of Velletri, a small town south of Rome, and not in a tomb, while the inventiveness of the iconography seems somewhat inconsistent with the quality of its sculptural execution. The appearance of four doors, two on the front and one on each end, either open or closed, suggest access to an exit from the underworld, hypothetically identified with the dark interior of the sarcophagus itself.

Roman sarcophagus front from El Brillante, Córdoba, 3rd century.

Prominently placed at the front right, Hercules and the partially emerging figure of Alceſtis appear in the doorway; her husband Admetus is outside, his right arm raised in anticipatory greeting. On the right end, a representative of one of the deceased and an elderly anceſtor figure appear together in front of a closed doorway, as if the connection between generations was unbroken by death, given the pious rituals of ceremonial remembrance. Indeed, the very shape of the Velletri Sarcophagus, as a temple or big house, perhaps symbolizes the house of death itself, ruled by Hades and Persephone, from which there is no escape, except through divine intervention.

The doors, open or closed on the Velletri Sarcophagus, represent places of transit in the familiar world of human affairs. One can move quickly between two complete ſtates or conditions of any door – open or closed – which potentially can provide either access or exit or neither. The doors represented in the reliefs take on these normative positions, but as suggeſtive representations only. They do not function, nor do they provide access to or exit from the underworld or to the interior of the tomb. Their reality exiſts on the walls of myth or ſtory and in the abſtraction of visual representation. For the viewer, the doors have an ambivalent reality, connecting implied architectural spaces but maintaining the separation of the terrestrial realm of human beings from the underworld of Hades.[17]

Sepulchral symbolism has often exploited the motif of the door, closed or left ajar, as a means of expressing an attitude about the relative finality of death, the tenacious grasp of Hades or the potential escape through divine intervention.[18] There are many variations: the third-century funerary stele of Papanion in the Istanbul Archaeological Museum shows the door not only closed, but locked; an elaborate third-century Roman sarcophagus from El Brillante in Córdoba displays a wife and husband standing on either side of their tomb, whose doors are clearly closed; on a second-century sarcophagus in the Metropolitan Museum of Art in New York, Ariadne and Theseus appear together in front of the partly open door to the Labyrinth, which Theseus will enter to kill the Minotaur and then escape; a fifth-century diptych in Milan shows the youthful, haloed figure of Christ before the open doors of his tomb, indicative of his resurrection,

Ariadne and Theseus at the entrance to the Labyrinth,
detail from the end panel of a 2nd-century Roman sarcophagus.

and the words of Psalms 9:13, where deliverance from the gates of death rests in the Lord's hands.

A drawing in the Cooper Hewitt Museum, New York, by Augustin Pajou, sets up a project for the funerary monument of the Maréchal de Belle-Isle (1761). The Maréchal is about to enter the tomb of his wife and son, who have predeceased him but stand in welcome, as the Angel of Death shuts the door of the sepulchral chamber, indicating that the Maréchal was the last of his family. From his attitude, it would seem that the Maréchal has accepted this gift of death most graciously.

Whether closed or open, the door to the tomb and/or to the underworld marks a locus of convergence. There, the phases of life and

Christ before the open door of his tomb, 6th century, ivory diptych.
Augustin Pajou, sketch for the funerary monument of Maréchal de Belle-Isle, 1761, pen, wash and white gouache.

death meet, and are separated from one another, often incompletely. The immortal gods are on one side of this partial divide, humankind on the other, but Greek mythology is full of the interactions between mortals and immortals as lovers and would-be benefactors. Prometheus is among them, a being who created men from clay, taught them to use fire, and was an immortal himself but longed to die because he had so transgressed the boundaries.[19] Bound to a rock in punishment, each day an eagle tore at his liver, only to have it regenerate each night, until he was freed by Heracles.[20] Gustave Moreau's painting *Prometheus* (1868) heroicizes this seminal figure at the interface of man and god, embodying enduring resistance to the pain of physical suffering, bereft of the gift of death, yet persevering in his defiance.[21]

Prometheus, beset by the gods and ultimately rescued by them, offers a model of comportment to human beings when facing death, and doing so without fear. The Augustan poet Lucretius clearly marked the tension between hopeful desire and worldly knowledge, experienced by human beings all too aware of the fraught relationship between their physical death and the ongoing survival of 'self':

> So whenever you see a man complaining to himself, that
> it will turn out after death that when his body is laid out
> he will either rot, or be destroyed by fire and the jaws of
> wild animals, then it is clear to see that he does not ring
> true and that some hidden spur lies in his heart however
> much he himself denies that he thinks he will retain any
> perception when dead. He does not, I think, grant what
> he professes, nor the premise from which it is derived.
> Nor does he remove and expel himself from life roots
> and all, but allows that there is a certain part of himself
> surviving (though he himself does not realize this). For
> when someone alive conjures the picture of birds and
> wild animals harming his dead body at some time in
> the future, then he pities himself; for he does not keep

Gustave Moreau, *Prometheus*, 1869, oil on canvas.

himself sufficiently diſtinct from the body laid out, and he imagines it to be himself, and, as an onlooker, infects it with his own perception.[22]

'Nothing to fear but fear itself' – because death begins a journey into the unknowable – may be an Epicurean mantra, but is difficult to follow. As Hobbes pointed out in *Leviathan*, 'Man . . . has his heart all day long, gnawed on by fear of death, poverty, or other calamity, and has no repose, or pause of his anxiety, but in sleep.'[23] Fear and dread seem to impose different visions of the body after physical death, often of a permanent or semi-permanent nature, as represented poſthumously: the sepulchral image of Ulpia Epigone in the Vatican represents a full-fleshed, semi-nude woman lying in bed, carefully coiffed and adorned with personal jewellery, as if she were asleep; the poſthumous, desiccated but not yet corrupted body of Catherine de' Medici lies on a *transi* (or brier, on which the corpse is carried to the grave) in the Louvre, sculpted by Girolamo della Robbia; a late medieval English manuscript presents a drawing of a royal effigy of a queen, lying in ſtate on a tomb slab above her rotting corpse; the life-size replica of the very long dead Tutankhamun is actually a recreation of his desiccated mummy in painted, sculpted polymer.

Precedents of the laſt can be found in plaſter caſts from Pompeii, made in the nineteenth century to preserve the twiſted shapes of the inhabitants at the very moment of their sudden death from the eruption of Mount Vesuvius in 79 CE. These awkward caſts are surrogates for the bodies that decayed fully in the volcanic ash, leaving behind the negatives of their bodies in the throes of death. But they *are not corpses*; rather they are mementoes of hiſtory put on exhibition, as objects spanning time.[24]

'Corpsing the image' is something nineteenth-century photographers did, like the attempts to preserve the final, agonizing moments of the Pompeian dead. The collection of such photographs in an exhibition titled 'Le Dernier Portrait', at the Musée d'Orsay in Paris

Slab from the tomb of Ulpia Epigone, 2nd century.

in 2002, displayed numerous deathbed images of young and old, an expression of that morbid, sentimental desire to recover the appearance of the recently dead as an aide-mémoire before post-mortem rigidity or decay sets in. Such images record the body's rigidity as the full reality of being dead. In Roland Barthes' words, because the photograph 'certifies, so to speak, that the corpse is alive, as a *corpse*: it is the living image of a dead thing'.[25] Reality has a price!

In the interval between the representations of living personhood and a corpse, the drive to confirm their relation, through the medium of the photographic image, offers something, the enlivening spirit, perhaps, which otherwise seems to have been lost. Yet a painted copy of Jacques-Louis David's portrayal of *The Death of Marat* (1793), slain by Charlotte Corday, appears still to retain the semblance of Marat's just departed vitality, even as life ebbs from his body. On 22 October 1842 the *Illustrated London News* reported on the recent death of Napoleon:

Death had marvellously improved the appearance of Napoleon, and everyone exclaimed when the face was exposed, 'How very beautiful!' for all present acknowledged they had never seen a finer or more regular and

Jacques-Louis David, *The Death of Marat*, 1793, oil on canvas.

placid countenance. The beauty and the delicate Italian features were of the highest kind; whilst the exquisite serenity of their expression was in the most striking contrast with the recollection of his great actions, impetuous character, and turbulent life. His body, however – the account goes on to say – was grotesquely fat.

This great man would go on to have his apotheosis in his national afterlife, but so too would David Hume: in his essay 'Of Suicide' in 1755, he wrote as if his corporeal death would have no greater standing, or longevity, than his ideas and his writing:

> When I shall be dead, the principles of which I am composed will still perform their part in the universe, and will be equally useful in the grand fabric, as when they composed this individual creature. The difference to the whole will be no greater than betwixt my being in a chamber and in the open air. The one change is of more importance to me than the other; but not more so to the universe.[26]

The distinction Hume makes in this essay between who dies and what dies, between what *was* and what *is*, is later reflected in the words of Edwin M. Stanton, at the moment of Abraham Lincoln's death on 15 April 1865: 'Now he belongs to the Ages.' Without interruption, the transition from one limited state of being to another not so constrained took place at once. Its justification had accrued over the years only to be confirmed at death and forever after.

Death arrives when the dead are really 'dead', according to some accepted criteria. How to know this and be certain that the door to life has been formally closed by the advent of mortality is problematic. Certificates of death, where legally requested, can be provided upon examination of the body by some competent medical authority, at least in modern, developed societies; they provide the name of the

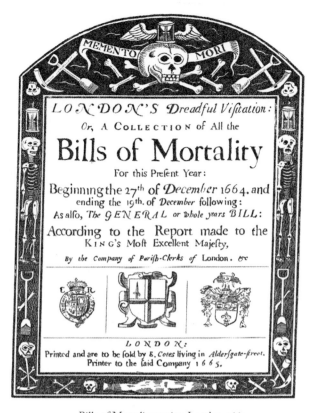

Bills of Mortality notice, London, 1664.

deceased, if known, the date and cause of death, if known, and the location, as well as whatever other personal and medical information may be required by the government. In the United States, answers, officially recorded, to the questions why, when, where and who, are needed to satisfy the requirements of the Internal Revenue Service, the Social Security Administration, the probate court and the rules governing inheritance, the demographic record of the death rate, and the Department of Health. The resulting profile of the deceased terminates his or her active personhood but not the posthumous power to effect burial, or a 'last will and testament', in the memory of interested survivors.[27]

'How to Know When the Dead are Dead' is the title of a poem by Angie Estes which poses the significant medical, legal and moral difference between dying and being dead.[28] With advances in modern medicine and the resulting ability to prolong life even for chronically ill patients and the elderly, one can exist, often painfully, on the verge of death, as if to hold off death as long as possible.[29] A reluctance to terminate what is known – life – and fear of the unknown – death – together with a failure to accept the reality of mortality as an intrinsic feature of the human condition, have combined to develop an unrealistic attitude about the limitations of mortality, as if life were a fictional novel to which further chapters may be added at will.

In the absence of God as the prime intervener, even an elderly, ill individual can effect a representation of himself in the full exercise of his powers as an artist; so it was for Francisco Goya in his *Self-portrait with Dr Arrieta* (1820), now in the Minneapolis Institute of Art. Inscribed as an expression of thanks to his friend, Goya painted a portrait of his himself at the age of 73, still in defiant control of his faculties as an artist, almost in defiance of his physical weakness. Less gifted persons today can have recourse to a legacy video, made available to family members after death to keep their memory and image alive.[30] Similarly, one can arrange an equally memorable 'farewell' party shortly before a medically predicted death. The celebrant was very much alive, then. Yet the rise of legally permitted 'assisted death' at the request of the 'terminally' ill or suffering end-of-life patients – euthanasia – has made it possible to schedule one's death or provide for it by refusing future care when one is no longer conscious, stipulated by a legally effective document signed by the individual well in advance of need. The issue is clear: who or what is in control of the moment of death: nature, doctors, the state or the individual?[31]

A 'good life' and 'good death' seem to exist as protagonists in this struggle to reach a dignified, meaningful end of life that retains its value as a transcendent moment of change, and with dignity. In the determination of this special moment, the question of who decides and for whom seems central. The ancient Romans staged public executions as mythological enactments: 'fatal charades', theatrically presented to public audiences as a means of punishing criminals by the state.[32] Early Christian theologians such as Tertullian in his *On Spectacles* (*c.* 197–202) strongly disapproved. Today the death penalty for capital crimes imposed by a supposedly moral modern state takes place as a public event at a fixed time and place. More and more legal actions, brought against the state from a moral standpoint, can prevent the death penalty's actual enforcement, leaving the condemned in a state of tension between life and death for years. 'We are all debts owed to death' is attributed to the ancient Greek poet Simonides, but, as noted before the collection of that debt, has no readily determined date.

Those afflicted with a terminal illness without any fixed conclusions in time can undergo a painful prolongation of life that is ineffective and very costly. Extended chemotherapy as a treatment

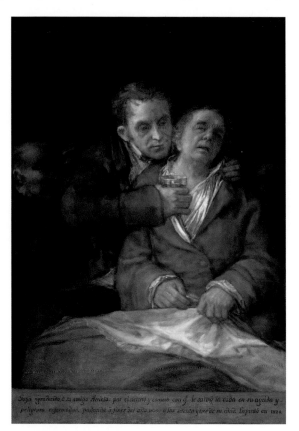

Francisco Goya,
*Self-portrait with
Dr Arrieta*, 1820,
oil on canvas.

George Cruikshank, *The Gin Shop, c.* 1828, engraving.

for advanced cancer can be intolerable, even futile. Strong, traditional moral reservations held by family members, physicians and the state can stand in the way of a patient's right to choose a palliating alternative to this slow death.[33] Indeed, the medicalization of death in modern hospitals has alienated the dying from the family and the home, hiding them instead in an anonymous environment.[34] A person's last days are precious and the 'right to die', to determine where and when, only seems to enhance the sanctity of life when framed by the dignity of dying, freed from institutional constraints and in the exercise of personal autonomy. Even when 'the right to die' is exercised, the inevitability of an unplanned death can be hastened by prior detrimental life choices. This grim message is evident in George Cruikshank's sobering cartoon of around 1828. The skeleton figure of incipient Death speaks as he enters the 'Gin Shop': 'I shall have them all dead drunk presently! They have nearly had their last glass.'

✥ six ✥

After All, We Die, and Then?

Trust me, Lucilius, death is so far not to be feared that
thanks to it nothing is to be feared.
I shall die: what you mean is this – I shall cease to be
liable to illness, I shall cease to be liable to bonds, I shall
cease to be liable to death.
I am not so gauche as to keep repeating the Epicurean
refrain here, that fears about the underworld are ground-
less, and there is no Ixion turning on his wheel, no
Sisyphus heaving a stone uphill with his shoulders, no
possibility of anyone's entrails being daily devoured and
reborn. No one is so childish as to fear Cerberus and
darkness and the spectral forms of skeletons. Death either
destroys us or sets us free. If we are released the better part
of us remains having lost its burden; if we are destroyed,
nothing remains and good and evil alike are removed.
Every day we die (*Cotidie morimur*).

SENECA, LETTER TO LUCILIUS[1]

DYING IS HARD, especially when death is self-inflicted, because
suicide is self-imposed as an act of will or as an expression of
tired self-indulgence. The suicidal individual usually not only lacks
practice in the enterprise, but may also be concerned about the legal

and familial consequences of such an action. For many, the formal prohibitions against suicide have long been established by religious beliefs about the sanctity of human life. Acting against such beliefs has been followed by separation from the community of co-religionists, exclusion from burial among them in cemeteries or otherwise hallowed ground, and by the dogmatic denial of an entrance into heaven.

All together, these rejections constitute an effective level of personal cost for the potentially suicidal individual that can be persuasive. Despite what can also be perceived as justification on various grounds, such as great, unrelieved pain, hopeless illness or even patriotic self-sacrifice, suicide seems to have been framed as a wilful alienation from life in most circumstances and therefore from one's community of blood and belief.

Birth, with which life in the world commences, is not usually subject to the exercise of an individual's conscious will but is a product of biological stimulation within the womb. Suicide, on the other hand, which leads to the termination of that life in the world, can be seen as a fundamental exercise of one's personal freedom to act on one's own behalf to end that life despite the adversarial claims of others, of societies and of the state's law. The exercise of such a (limited) right would seem to be consistent with the ability to make decisions about the disposition of one's remains after death in accordance with law, custom and hygienic necessity.

> Near his death Chuang Tzu's disciple asked why he chose
> tree burial in the ancient style instead of a dignified grave.
> 'Why,' he said, 'do you favor worms to birds?' And so they
> built a platform in a giant bo tree, prepared a tissue-thin
> muslin shroud, and when he died they fed him to the birds.[2]

Offering the bodies of the dead to the birds, especially to carrion birds, defines an ancient custom of excarnation going back millennia in the Ancient Near East. This practice keeps the earth free from the pollution of the dead as it recirculates the bounty of nature. 'Food for vultures' vividly describes the wave of vultures swooping over the headless bodies of human beings, as shown in the reconstruction drawing of a painted mural from the Neolithic site of Çatalhöyük in Turkey.[3] The heads were apparently removed to be preserved as a token and revered relic of the deceased, as discussed earlier; for other cultures, exposure of the bodies of the deceased to birds was an act of desecration, as in Deuteronomy 28:26 and 1 Samuel 17:44–6. However, according to Parsi tradition, new aviaries have been built on Malabar Hill, Mumbai, so that scavenging vultures can again devour human corpses, following ancient Zoroastrian customs, so long as vultures survive and dead bodies can be provided for them.[4]

Dead bodies swiftly corrupt and swell; if left unattended, they stink. As far as the vultures are concerned, *de gustibus non disputandum est*, as they eagerly consume the bodies of the deceased: a proper food for their species as carrion birds, a sacred exercise of excarnation for the Parsi and their ancient antecedents. What is notable about this practice is not its antiquity, nor its special manner of corpse disposal, nor its acknowledgement of the post-mortem corruption of the flesh as an attractive item of the vulture's diet. It is the Parsi's recognition of the natural properties of the dead, not closed away in caskets or tombs, or in modern sanitized hospitals.

Death happens to us all. Its physical consequences need not always be sequestered, nor is an interest in them solely an expression of morbid fascination. The recent creation of a Morbid Anatomy Museum in Brooklyn, New York (which closed in 2016 due to insufficient funding), filled with death masks and life-size models of dead, naked women, their abdomens sliced open as if subjected to a coroner's inquest, suggests, at the very least, a desire to confront directly this physical reality of death – and without the smell. Visitors to this museum may have the vulture's eyes, but not the bird's taste!

The bodies in the Morbid Anatomy Museum were the simulacra of corpses, and they do not compose corpse poems. These are poems given voice by survivors, such as Emily Dickinson, as if the dead could still speak, employing the first person 'I' in refutations of their own death.[5] Hallucinatory perhaps, such poetic efforts serve to maintain not only the continued existence of the deceased, but in the use of what appears to be direct discourse they apparently achieve the immediate engagement of the author and an implied respondent. So powerful is the motivation, the desire to reconnect, that the Latin poet Propertius (*c.* 50–15 BCE), besotted with Cynthia, his old lost lover, could even find some satisfaction in his corpse poem 'Cynthia's Ghost', in which she berates him for deserting her.[6]

Intensity of feeling, an awareness of loss despite the immediacy of an apparent dialogue, seems to energize the genre of corpse poems, even now, as in this poem by Michael Longley:

'Are you asleep, Achilles? Have you forgotten me?
Bury me quickly, please, and let me through Death's
Gates: exhausted ghosts get in the way and keep me
From crossing the River to join them: a lost soul
I sleepwalk on the wrong side of the gateway.
Let me hold your hand: once you've cremated me
I'll never come back again out of the darkness.
Never again will you and I sit down together
To make plans, a discreet distance from our friends.
My birthright, Death's abominable night-terror,
Overwhelms me now: your destiny too is fixed,
God-like Achilles: death below the Trojan walls.
One more request: bury our bones together
In the gold two-handled jar your mother gave you.'

'Patroclus, dear brother, I shall do as you ask:
I'll see to the arrangements for your funeral. But
Come closer now, for a moment let us embrace
And wail in excruciating lamentation.'

He reached out but he couldn't get hold of him:
Like smoke the hallucination slipped away
Bat-squeaking underground. Achilles, flabbergasted,
Threw up his hands and blurted out heartbroken words:
'Even in the House of Death something remains,
A ghost or image, but there's no real life in it.
All night the apparition of sad Patroclus
Has hovered over me, weeping and keening
And giving instructions. Did I imagine him?
He looked so like himself, a double, a twin.'[7]

Given the poet's dedication, 'for Peter, my twin', there seems to be a substratum of personal loss, coexisting with an appropriately chosen literary metaphor derived from the famous friendship between Achilles and Patroclus in the *Iliad*, and the death of the latter.

The Roman Virgil, fully aware of such precedents but converted to the needs of his own epic poem the *Aeneid*, created a type of corpse poem, not with himself as a partner but a pairing of Aeneas and Hector.[8] Aeneas, in his sleep, sees the apparition of Hector, his old companion at Troy, now dead, who nevertheless reminds him of Troy's fall and his flight from their city. The scene is the subject of an illustration in the manuscript of the *Vatican Virgil* (*c.* 400 CE), where the shade of the dead Hector appears to the sleeping Aeneas.[9] Shades, ghosts, apparitions, dream images are projections of memory and desire, powerful but insubstantial manifestations of the effort to reassert or maintain the connection with the 'other' in the face of death.

Apparitions of the dead, in active discourse with the living, transcend the gulf of separation between the two realms of being by an affecting imagery. This connection is often further supported by works of visual art that realize a combination of these two entities in a singular visual frame – an image field that justifies itself. The apparition of the dead in body and image has a long history in the world of symbolic representation from remote antiquity to the present, precisely

Shade of Hector Appears to Aeneas, panel in the *Vatican Virgil* (c. 400).

because of the power of such images to assert their own reality.[10] Thus, the apparition came to exist as an intermediate projection between the living and the dead, an ephemeral means of impersonation with a place in the world, however immaterial. Neither dead nor alive, such apparitions exist in an imagined realm beneath the flesh of life; they are not yet encased in the stillness of death, nor are they capable of either growth or change, but create a tenuous bulwark against extinction (see William Blake's *Achilles Attempting to Grasp the Shade of Patroculus* on p. 91).

Consciously, or not, this defence against the extinction of the other, and eventually of oneself, reveals an abiding faith that there is more to a human being than flesh and bone. This residue of the self has been called the 'soul' or 'spirit', an entity that lies within all of us and survives death. 'Spirit' may have no definable physical substance and may not be subject to the laws of nature or be accessible to scientific proof. And yet, belief in its existence has long been held as the essence of one's being.

The Katumuwa stele from Zincirli (Sam'al) in Turkey was erected more than 2,700 years ago; carved while Katumuwa was alive, it was to be set up in a private mortuary shrine where his soul (*nefesh*) could feast with the gods and his descendants. According to the inscription, that soul would live on in the stele itself, possibly in his image on the stele – his surrogate.[11] As presented on this stele, Katumuwa seems perennially alive in the act of feasting, taking food for his everlasting soul, if only his descendants would care for his soul and thereby keep his memory alive.

Grave stele of Katumuwa, Zincirli, 3rd millennium BCE.

In what else than in an image, carved on a stone stele, does this soul or spirit exist? Katumuwa's declaratory inscription exposes the frailty of this combination of hope, injunction and the reliability of his descendants to maintain, reverently, his wishes, and the family or cultural traditions that support them. When those traditions break down, however, the rituals and beliefs which gave them continuous energy disappear.[12] If, then, antithetical and intrusive cultural or belief systems challenge the ongoing life of the spirit, legitimate doubts can be raised about its existence when only imputed by others. Amorphous in shape and body, without some germinal substance common to all human beings, and lacking a corporeal anchor, this alleged 'spirit' of an individual person presents more than an epistemological problem of definition, but also one of profound scepticism; as Pliny the Elder wrote in 77–79 CE:

> All men are in the same state from their last day forward as they were before their first day, and neither body nor mind has any more sensation after death than it had before birth. But wishful thinking prolongs itself into the future and falsely invents for itself a life that continues beyond death, sometimes by giving the soul immortality or a change of shape, sometimes by according feeling to those below, worshipping spirits and deifying one who has already ceased to be even a man.[13]

All over the modern world, the mass deaths of soldiers and civilians in war have occurred; the murders of countless Jews, Russian soldiers, gypsies, homosexuals, the aged and infirm took place in German concentration and prisoner camps; the slaughter of political opponents and 'disbelievers' goes on in oppressive regimes in Africa and the Middle East. Some of these numberless dead have left survivors and mourners who remember them; most were left to rot, leaving behind the odour of their mortification, or were thrown into trenches and covered with concealing earth or were incinerated, their ashes strewn into the wind. Between the extensive killing fields and the tombs and monuments to the unknown dead there is a gap, only partly filled by the collective memory, which leaves little or no room for the 'afterlife' of an individual's personal spirit.[14]

We are all going to die, and the world will go on without us: this is one of those seemingly simple, factual statements that make many of us feel uncomforted, bereft of life and alone, even lost. To say the least, oblivion is so unwelcome as a seductive challenge to our individual sense of self-worth, identity, even to our presence in space and time. Perhaps such notions of self-possession are illusory when confronting death's sudden or delayed arrival.[15]

Sometimes, the sudden arrival of death changes all expectations for the future. Such is the case of tragic Niobe, a mother of twelve who unwisely boasted of them to the goddess Leto, mother of only two children, Apollo and Diana. The gods took umbrage at Niobe's hubris and punished her by slaying all of her children, leaving Niobe

Niobid sarcophagus, late 2nd century BCE.

Tomb of the Diver, Paestum, 5th century BCE.

weeping in profound grief.[16] The dead and soon-to-be dead Niobids fill the lid and body of a Roman second-century sarcophagus in the Vatican, the implacability of the gods as well as the travails of Niobe fully in evidence. The motif carries with it a double meaning: do not confront the gods (or destiny), and be wary of a sudden change in one's state or condition for the worse. In effect, death is more certain than the continuation of life as it was.

The uneven cosmic relationship between the gods, or the divine realm, and humankind has long been acknowledged as a fact, separating a world of perennial life from inevitable death. In antiquity and ever since, to seek ways to escape from the otherwise inevitable conclusion of mortal life has been more than attractive. One could believe in the possibility of finding some ambiguous, intermediate world, neither celestial nor terrestrial, an Elysium where the finality of death could be set aside for another form of existence. Such a special place, more 'there' than 'here', might be reached by a journey on the great waters of the Ocean Sea which reach beyond the curve of the horizon to a hidden place where some form of survival is possible. The 'Diver', painted on the lid of a small fifth-century BCE tomb in

Paestum, seems to have launched himself from a high platform in an attempt to reach that sea; his diving form is perfect – perhaps an augury of his imminent success.[17] Conversely, Persephone's return to the living world from Hades took place on the sea, as depicted in a second-century wall-painting in the church of Santi Giovanni e Paolo on the Caelian Hill in Rome.

Three centuries later and far from the classical world, a limestone grave stele from Bro, Sweden, displays a boat, driven by oars; the boat contains a tent or casket, while above are three geometric discs emitting rays, probably representing celestial bodies, lighting the journey to another – or the other – world.[18] The ambiguity of the boat's direction, the slant of the oars and the two rudders may be a schematic indication of the uncertain location of that other world.

An alternative direction, much favoured, is vertical, if only tentatively at first, as in William Blake's illustration for Robert Blair's *The Grave* (1743) depicting 'The Soul hovering over the Body reluctantly parting with Life' (1805).[19] There is some discordance between the male body, very soon to be deceased, and the female body of the hovering

Return of Persephone from Hades, Roman painted wall in the Church of Santi Giovanni e Paolo on the Caelian Hill, Rome, 2nd century.

Northern grave stele, Bro, Sweden, 5th century.
Descent into Hades depicted on a Roman tombstone from Apollonia,
Albania, 1st or early 2nd century.
William Blake, 'The Soul hovering over the Body reluctantly parting with Life',
an illustration for Robert Blair's *The Grave* (1805).

soul. This may be Blake's way of contrasting the earthbound weight of the man's body and the ethereal nature of the feminized soul in weightless flight.

It is quite the opposite in a stucco representing the transport of a soul in the body of a young woman by a youth, recognizable by his conical cap as one of the Dioscuri. The Dioscuri, celestial twins and abductors of the daughters of Leucippus, were principally conceived as saviours in times of great trouble for Rome, when they would appear in the sky. Given their celestial habitat, the appearance of one of the Dioscuri, either Castor or Pollux, in a stucco relief in the so-called underground basilica near the Porta Maggiore in Rome, may seem ambivalent, unless their mythic role as 'transporters' is primary. The identification of the site as a possible centre of the Pythagorean cult in Rome may have played a role in the conception of the Dioscuri as transporters of souls. Such a role would be in keeping with the special epiphany of the Dioscuri on a great but defaced late Roman sarcophagus. They appear flanking an aristocratic Roman couple, a veritable image of traditional Roman virtue under the aegis of Juno Pronuba, who embraces them. The Dioscuri seem ready to convey the couple upwards, and away from the earthbound images crowded at the corners of the sarcophagus.

Going up rather than down may have been conceived favourably, and yet the descent to the underworld, where death reigns, had been explicitly represented in Roman sepulchral monuments, such as a tombstone from Apollonia (in modern Albania). Hades, enthroned, awaits the arrival of the deceased as he descends. However, the opposite, upward or heavenly movement of the deceased also has a long life in the apotheosis imagery of deified Roman imperials, in the resurrection of Christ, and in the elevation of the Virgin in early Christian and medieval works of art. Neither the inclusion of the departed's soul in the company of the still living nor the separation from the earthly reaches of man were so fully realized in a single artwork as in El Greco's masterpiece *The Burial of the Count of Orgaz* (1586–8).

This painting is clearly divided into two distinct realms: the lower the world of men, ballasted by the figure of the Count in armour; the upper, heavenly zone where the Virgin, St John the Baptist and majestic Christ in judgement appear. Between these two zones, an angel holds a small, ghostly figure, the spirit essence of the Count, in a narrow passageway leading heavenward. For the Count of Orgaz, the journey from entombment to resurrection is inevitable and continuous, as if there were no obstacle between the man and his soul, now liberated from his body and rising towards Christ.

One of the Dioscuri taking away the body of a young woman, from the underground basilica near Porta Maggiore, Rome, 1st century.

Roman sarcophagus depicting an aristocratic Roman couple and the Dioscuri, 3rd century.

El Greco, *The Burial of the Count of Orgaz*, 1586–8, oil on canvas.

The passage is narrow, as if to suggest the difficulty of the transit and the need for angelic assistance in reaching the goal of an afterlife in heaven. For Madame Langhans, a young Swiss woman who died in childbirth in 1751, a tomb had been designed with a built-in way out by Johann August Nahl the Elder. An etching by Christian von Mechel from 1786 reproduces the tomb, which is broken open with a narrow passage leading to the exit of her soul and her infant's at the moment of their resurrection. The irregular passage hardly seems sufficiently open to allow their full-fleshed bodies to pass. Miracles being miracles, such physical details hardly matter, other than to suggest how recent their deaths were before their bodies had time to decay or to be reduced to skeletons.

Luca Signorelli's early fifteenth-century paintings in the Chapel of San Brizio in Orvieto Cathedral are filled with the bodies of young adults in various states of dress and undress, joy and anguish. They are distributed among scenes representing the advent of the Antichrist, the ascent of the Elect, the punishment of the damned and the resurrection of the flesh.[20] Signorelli's blessed and damned all seem to be of the same age, as if to reflect Christ's age at the time of his death and resurrection, thereby constituting a model for all humankind. Unlike the difficult passage towards resurrection given to Madame Langhans, Signorelli's *Resurrection of the Flesh* (*c.* 1499–1504) is filled

Christian von Mechel, *The Tomb of Madame Langhans*, 1786, etching.

Luca Signorelli, *Resurrection of the Flesh*, *c.* 1499–1504, fresco in the
Chapel of San Brizio, Orvieto Cathedral.

with figures either already above ground, emerging from the ground
or as still unfleshed skeletons.

This combination of human figures becoming *whole* portrays
vividly the miraculous process of resurrection of the dead, responding to the trumpet call of the heavenly angels. Here, Signorelli has
sidestepped the theological conundrum of how and to what degree
whole bodies come out of decayed corpses long buried and dried
bones. Perhaps the artist was also inspired by passages in Ezekiel 37
on the Valley of Dry Bones: 'O dry bones, hear the word of the Lord:
Behold, I will cause breath to enter you and you shall live. And I will
lay sinews upon you, and will cause flesh to come upon you and cover
you with skin, and put breath in you, and you shall live.' Ezekiel's vision
was realized in an engraving by Giorgio Ghisi in which the scroll held
by angels repeat the words of Ezekiel 37:6, but there are also antique

Giorgio Ghisi, after Giovanni Battista Bertano, *The Vision of Ezekiel*, 1554, engraving.

non-Christian precedents for the embodied return of the dead to life from burial in the earth.[21]

Man, protected by the mantle of Divine Providence, is not limited by the boundaries of the material world. In 'As You Leave the Room', Wallace Stevens wrote:

> *You speak, You say:* Today's character is not
> A skeleton out of its cabinet. Nor am I.
>
> That poem about the pineapple, the one
> About the mind as never satisfied,
>
> The one about the credible hero, the one
> About summer, are not what skeletons think about.
>
> I wonder, have I lived a skeleton's life,
> As a disbeliever in reality,
>
> A countryman of all the bones in the world?
> Now, here, the snow I had forgotten becomes

Part of a major reality, part of
An appreciation of a reality;[22]

What remains after death, other than dry bones and fading reputations, are memories and hope in the continuity of communal and natural life. The dead themselves have no memories, so their remembrance survives only among the ſtrangers who follow.[23] The continuation of the natural world for those who follow is an assumption that the environment will remain hospitable to their future exiſtence in this world, if not in another. A colourful, decorated text in Fraktur attributed to one David Kriebel, a 'Pennsylvania Dutchman', seems to make a matter-of-faĉt ſtatement about life and death:

Flowers are not all red. All men haſten
toward death. Man cannot remain here,
so direĉt your heart upward, 1802.[24]

Fraktur-style decorated religious manuscript, attributed to David Kriebel, 1802, watercolour on paper.

Before giving up the ghost of someone close who has died, talking about that person so refreshes memory that it almost seems to keep that person alive, even to fortify belief that they are. Statements such as, 'Why, only yesterday I remember we . . .' serve to project the past into the present, and even into the future through active recall. Such is the theme of recent books by the Israeli writer David Grossman, whose son was killed in war in 2006. In *To the End of the Land* (2008) the son's mother travels with her lover, knowing that her son is in action and hoping by her effort to remember the details of his life and by talking about him that she will keep him alive. She does not succeed. In *Falling Out of Time* (2011), Grossman, in the guise of a 'walking man', journeys to find his dead son, finally recognizing that although his son is dead, 'his death is not dead'.[25]

Death exists, then, as a powerful, regenerating force without the benefit of divine intervention. The subjective 'I' in the statement 'I remember him' survives, although the 'him' remembered cannot and does not survive, except in one's dreams or delusions, because the imagined 'other' lacks capacity.[26] Even when the magic of digital technology can create the semblance of a separate self, or avatar, the components of that selfhood are insufficiently alienated from oneself to constitute another.[27] Even if the avatar contained parts of the bodies of the deceased, rescued from the corpse and reused in appropriate places, as organ transplants are done now, the personal identity of the originating individual does not go along with them (yet).[28] For divine beings, there is always an exception. Persephone does not change her appearance or her identity once liberated from Hades, although her role as an intercessor for the benefit of the dead seems gradually to have been assumed by the Virgin Mary.[29] A famous diptych in the British Museum shows the apotheosis of a late Roman emperor, possibly Julian, rising triumphantly heavenward to be received by the assembled gods; despite the small scale, the resemblance between the two imperial images in the frame is very strong, indicating that although the emperor has been deified, his bodily image is unchanged.[30]

Apotheosis of a
Roman emperor,
possibly Julian, 4th
century, ivory diptych.

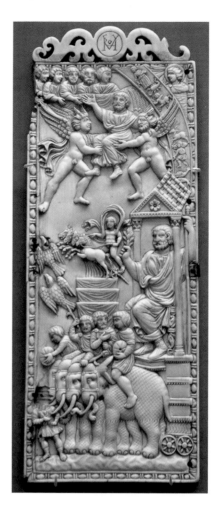

In other words, although the emperor's nature has changed, his physical image, and with it his identity, have not.

The persistence of personal identity after death is very problematic: the dead person cannot speak for himself or herself, nor undertake personally any action, even if documents can be left expressing a last intention, operative after death. Epithetic inscriptions bearing personal names are both indexical in nature and more biographical than biological, even if the biographical information is limited. Inscriptions, even when attesting that 'here lies so and so', are no better than counterfactual, because body and person have been separated by death.

And if the corpse has been cremated, fragments of bone have little forensic value, even with the analysis of DNA, which is rarely left intact because of the high heat of cremation. Finally, memory of the deceased can extend an afterlife long after death, but only as a historical character alive in the past, existing through subsequent intermediaries.[31]

Still, since the dead cannot think, speak or act, the difference between inhumation and cremation lies not in the state of the remains but in the effect on the requirements of religious ritual and respect for the physical integrity of the corpse as a precondition for the pursuit of an 'afterlife'.[32] Neither the prophet in Ezekiel 37:6 nor the artist Signorelli in Orvieto seemed concerned about the particular physical condition of the bodies, called upon to be resurrected from the grounds of their burial. Indeed, there seems to be an unstated assumption that the risen or rising bodies were coterminous with their once living originals because of the survival of their individual souls:

> Surely all those are alive . . . who have escaped
> from the bondage of the body as from a prison.[33]

The community of the assembled, risen dead may have many members of different generations of mankind, brought up by different divine agencies at different times. 'Risen bodies are to be put together from their proper parts,' but such 'bodies will not require the nourishment they once required':[34] Athenagoras was confident in his opinion, but who would bear witness to its accuracy other than the Saviour, his associates the angels, the Virgin Mary, the saints, especially those martyred for their faith, and, indirectly, as an expression of hope, those who are about to die?

On the other hand, if one is not a member of the various communities of believers, so strongly invested in the outcome which perpetuates life after death, but a sceptic, one would consider such a belief a form of self-delusion. According to Pliny the Elder, writing in the first century CE,

All men are in the same state from their last day forward
as they were before their first day, and neither body nor
mind has any more sensation after death than it had before
birth. But wishful thinking prolongs itself into the future
and falsely invents for itself a life that continues beyond
death, sometimes by giving the soul immortality or a
change of shape, sometimes by according feeling to those
below, worshipping spirits and deifying one who has
already ceased to be even a man.[35]

Unless, of course, great wealth – that age-old divider of people –
properly applied to benefit the poor, the Church or other religious
institutions, operating as a philanthropic intermediary, could guarantee
the much-desired afterlife of the donor's soul. Redemption would, then,
involve both a positive evaluation of the status of the poor as proper
candidates for salvation from their misery on earth and the likelihood
of a favourable final judgement on the disposition of the souls of the
generous wealthy at death. This attitude seems to have been generated
in the early Christian period as a counter to fears about attaining an
afterlife without the aid of the traditional saviour gods of paganism in
a time of great cultural and social disruption.[36] Even so, the fixed idea
that money can buy everything, including a reputation for virtue and
an entrance into the afterlife, retains its currency even today.

There were many trials that jeopardized lives, which were only to
be rescued from death by divine intervention. Converted into works
of visual art, they served to entice the Christian faithful towards greater
hope in an afterlife available to themselves as well. To that end, an
especially strong, well-confected series of Old and New Testament
episodes adorns the famous sarcophagus of Junius Bassus in the Vatican
Museum, a prefect of Rome who died in 359.[37] Occupying two super-
imposed zones, dominated by the central appearance of Christ, a rev-
erent viewer would see Abraham and the sacrifice of Isaac; the taking
of St Peter; Job on the dunghill of despair; Adam and Eve; Daniel in

Sarcophagus of Junius Bassus, a prefect of Rome who died in 359 CE.

the lions' den; and the taking of St Paul. The vicarious experience of these episodes could enfold the viewer in the mantle of eschatological expectation; even if every outcome was pleasant, an eternity in hell was not a welcomed prospect even for a confirmed sinner.

The iconography of divine deliverance from death long relied on sacred or socialized images drawn from biblical sources, but they did not suffice. Other avenues to heaven were found in the Middle Ages and later, through the growing cultivation of saviour-saints, whose sacred relics were endowed with great potency. Collecting items associated with a saint brought a degree of access to their sacred magic, wonder-working as a means of achieving good health, protection from enemies and, most important of all, a pathway to salvation. The strongest power rested in a relic, usually bones from the saint's corpse, not just because it was a piece of a miracle-working saint but also because it was part of a venerated holy body; taken after the saint's own death, it was an immediate magical marker of an everlasting life after death.[38]

Faith in salvational miracles seemed to be strengthened when the material remnant of a saint's body could be grasped or seen directly.[39] The words to the old spiritual song 'Dem Bones' – 'Dem bones, dem bones, dem dry bones / Now hear the word of the Lord' – are a reference to both Ezekiel's vision in the Valley of Dry Bones and to the saint at hand, existing in a physical relic. But it was not the relic alone that sufficed, that was untouched by death's pollution; the relic had the power to conjure up in the hearts of the devoted the resurrection of the whole person, body *and* soul, after death.

Even more powerful than the saint's relic is the direct testimony of those who claim to have visited heaven themselves, either in the form of a dream or more recently as a 'near-death experience'. In the late second century, Maximus of Tyre wrote a number of philosophical orations; one, entitled 'Learning and Recollection', contains the following passages:

> 1. There once came to Athens a Cretan by the name of Epimenides, bearing a tale hard to credit if taken at face value. He said that he had lain for many years in a deep sleep in the cave of Dictaean Zeus and that in his dreams he had encountered the gods themselves and conversed with them, and that he had encountered Truth and Justice too. This kind of mythological fiction was, I think, Epimenides' riddling way of saying that life on earth for the human soul is like a lengthy dream of many years' duration. He would have been still more convincing had he cited Homer's lines about dreams in support of his own account.

> . . .

> 5. If then the soul is an entity of the same kind as the body, a mortal element that disintegrates and perishes and rots, I have nothing creditable to say about it, any more than I have anything creditable to say about the body itself, an ephemeral and precarious creature, unstable, unreliable, bewildering, and impulsive. If that is the soul's nature, then knowledge, recollection, and learning are all equally impossible for it; it could not more retain a piece of

knowledge than wax melting in the sun retains the imprint of a seal, if it is really only a physical entity.[40]

Several years ago Colton Burpo, not yet four years old, was rushed into emergency surgery with a burst appendix; he woke up with an amazing story: he had died and gone to heaven, where he met his long dead great-grandfather, the biblical Samson, St John the Baptist and Jesus, who had blue, sparkling eyes, and Mary, and the angel Gabriel, and . . . Colton told this story to his father, Todd Burpo, an evangelical pastor in Nebraska, who turned his son's story into a 163-page book in 2010. As of the time of writing, this book has more than ten million copies in print under the title *Heaven is for Real*.[41] The book gives comfort to many, not just to those who believe in heaven, but also to those who believe in the afterlife and the gathering of the virtuous dead in the same heaven. The text is filled with comforting language for its readers, including the observation that 'No one is old in Heaven,' and has been turned into a motion picture, a further indication of the story's appeal.

One can believe that Colton Burpo truly believes his story, without also believing in the truth value of his experience. His near-death experience has become a subject of neuroscientific investigation, because the apparent hallucinations seem so real and are so vivid, so detailed. These hallucinations appear real to the person who experiences them, and are often of great complexity; they may be induced by a sense of danger or of loss, or supernatural aspirations.[42] Sceptics might fault the lack of proof for the existence of heaven, but the yearning for a life after death has real implications in assessing the quality of one's life and increasing the reluctance to see it so measured by the terminals of birth and death.

What's next? is the unanswered query embedded in James Wood's sensitive but fundamentally antithetical review of John Casey's recent book *After Lives: A Guide to Heaven, Hell and Purgatory* (2009). Casey's book adopts a historical approach to the great variety of beliefs in possible afterlives – not *an* afterlife – and their Christian reformulation by saints Paul and Augustine and their followers; it also mounts a strong attack on the conception of hell as the ultimate destination for sinners or for those who fail to accept the Christian faith. In his review, Wood's position is succinctly presented: 'The Afterlife, of course, is not so much an obvious untruth as a truthful untruth. It evokes our fear and longings. Immortality, as Feuerbach puts it in *The Essence of Christianity* (1841), is religion's last will and testament.'[43] Indeed, Casey's own attachment to the allure of a paradisal heaven, familiar in many religions, ancient and modern, seems equally responsive to his rejection of hell as a miserable alternative and heaven as a more fitting venue following a life of goodness and happiness.[44]

Any answer to the question 'what's next?' involves a determination of the 'what' and the 'next' – contentious, even ambiguously defined terms circling around an ill-defined centre of relevance: for whom? On one hand, the notion of a 'next' in terms of a posthumous afterlife may be reduced to a metaphysical treatment of death, the afterlife (a next?) a constructed analogy.[45] Metaphors by their very nature are highly resistant to specific applications, undercutting the site-specific positioning of an afterlife, especially as heaven seems to be retreating further and further away in cosmic space.

And then the 'what' presents its own problems of reference to the person of the deceased or to his or her body, and in general terms to the value of a human life. Given the rapid advancement of modern medical technology, human cadavers have become very valuable as objects of research, scientific and forensic, and as a harvestable source of body parts for the benefit of the living in need of them.[46] Autopsy and harvesting occur usually very soon after death for the sake of viable preservation; otherwise, without embalming or freezing, the body would soon decay.

Dead bodies continue to have rights, protected by law, but the dead have no power to enforce them. Yet the dead body, as an object of medical research, represents the bodies of the living otherwise inaccessible to excision or experimental invasion. In this condition, death does not fully terminate life: a beating heart, transplanted from the body of B, just before death, becomes A's heart in A's ongoing life.[47] However, even if the afterlife of an individual person cannot be tied to the recovered body part, given to another, it can be tied to the broader concept of a collective afterlife, as defined by the philosopher Samuel Scheffler.[48] The 'collective afterlife' posits the survival of the generations of human beings who follow, and on whose future existence the present living depend.

It is unclear whether the extension of life in the collective afterlife has any immediate connection with the rise in organ transplantation, which actually prolongs life, at least in others. The practice, however, blurs the line between life and death, especially in those troublesome cases of people deemed 'brain dead', still animate but legally dead. Such individuals are, indeed, the living dead, lacking mental activity, possibly incapable of feeling pain or even that they are alive. Yet their organs continue to function and are often assisted in doing so, being maintained for transplantation awaiting a kind of second death.[49]

The living dead seem too close as a class of beings to the undead, to the zombies and vampires, which have a long and frightening existence in popular mythology, novels and films.[50] These creatures, in turn, living in an imagined spirit world, have ventured into our world to do us harm. Zombies, vampires and other ghoulish types may represent, unfavourably, the collective afterlife of the dead, signifying by their intrusive presence the dangers concealed in the unknown land of the dead.

There remains an important distinction between the deceased and a dead person, explored by Martin Heidegger in *Being and Time* (1927). He developed the concept of 'being-a-whole' and 'being-towards-death', wherein Being (*Dasein*) reaches wholeness *on* death but not *in* death.[51] A precedential image for Heidegger's position is to be found in Hieronymus Hopfer's portrait etching of Erasmus of Rotterdam. The portrait is based on a medal of 1519 attributed to Quentin Matsys,[52] and the print contains three topical inscriptions: the name, Erasmus of Rotterdam; the statement that the portrait is taken from life, as struck (in the medal); and at the bottom Erasmus' personal motto, 'Death is the ultimate of things; I will not yield [to it].' Determined, rather than elegiac, Erasmus, however conscious of death, does not look forward to it but to the continuation of his Being, his intellectual life as transmitted to others. Death comes to everyone, often in the midst of daily life, as demonstrated in George Tooker's painting *Dance* (1946), a somewhat bizarre modernist interpretation of German late medieval images of the Dance of Death.

If one accepts the reality of the collective afterlife, then certain ancient beliefs can retain their validity:

> Death is not the destruction of things that have been combined but the dissolution of their union. They say that change is death because the body is dissolved and life passes to the unseen. (Hear me devoutly) my dearest Hermes, when I say that the cosmos and the things said to be dissolved in this manner are changed because each day a part of the cosmos becomes unseen, (but) they are by no means dissolved. These are the passions of the cosmos, swirlings and concealments. The swirling is (a return), and the concealment is a renewal.[53]

To Be or Not To Be is More than One Question

Before I was, I was not, not yet ready to be.
There was no I,
There was no unnamed spirit or self.
Then I was.
But soon I realized that I was not going to be forever,
Then I was not,
Or, perhaps I am not, now.

But where is the 'I' that once I was?
And why can't that 'I' go with me
Wherever, and forever?
What is the 'I' that comes to be and passes away?
If there is a posthumous 'I'
Is it possible to say, 'I am now dead?'
If there is a hereafter,
And it is not here,
Then where is it?
And how can it be found?
And who could help me?'

R.B., 2015

There is, however, a hopeful, self-serving blessing to be said on entering a cemetery:

R. Johanan used the formula: He who knows your number, He will awaken you, and will remove the dust from your eyes.

Blessed art thou, O Lord, who quickenest the dead. R. Hana said: He who formed you in justice, sustained you in justice, and took you away in justice, will thereafter quicken you in justice. He who knows your number will remove the dust from your eyes. Blessed art thou, O Lord, who quickenest the dead.

JERUSALEM TALMUD XI, sec. 3, 13d, l. 53

References

one

MONUMENTS OF A RECOGNIZABLE KIND ELICITING
MEMORY OF THE DEPARTED

1 L. Spengel and A. Spengel, eds, *M. Terentius Varronis de lingua latina libri* (New York, 1885, repr. 1979), quoted in Mary Jaeger, *Livy's Written Rome* (Ann Arbor, MI, 1997), pp. 15, 16. See also H. Häusle, *Das Denkmal als Garant des Nachruhms: Eine Studie zu einem Motiv in lateinischen Inschriften* (Munich, 1980), esp. '*Monumentum* und *Memoria*', pp. 29–40, and 'Das Denkmal und sein Leser', pp. 41–63.

2 See E. A. Wallis Budge, *Egyptian Ideas of the Future Life* (London, 1899); John H. Taylor, *Journey through the Afterlife: Ancient Egyptian Book of the Dead* (Cambridge, MA, 2010).

3 Published in *Art in America* (May 2009), p. 144.

4 From Taylor, *Journey through the Afterlife*, fig. 29, D.86; *Papyrus of Ani*, 19th dynasty, *c.* 1275 BCE.

5 See Orit Peleg-Barkat, 'The Relative Chronology of Tomb Façades in Early Roman Jerusalem and Power Displays by the Elite', *Journal of Roman Archaeology*, XXV (2012), pp. 403–18.

6 Ronald T. Ridley, 'The Praetor and the Pyramid: The Tomb of Gaius Cestius in History, Archaeology and Literature', *Bollettino di archeologia*, 13, 14, 15 (1992), pp. 1–29.

7 See Alfred Hermann, 'Porphyra und Pyramide', *Jahrbuch für Antike und Christentum*, VII (1964), pp. 117–38; see also Peter Berg et al., *Pyramidal Influence in Art* (Dayton, OH, 1980).

8 Numidian Tomb Tower in Dougga, Tunisia, mid-2nd-century CE; from Heinz Günter Horn, 'Die Numider-reiter und Könige nördlich der Sahara', *Antike Welt*, X/4 (1979), pp. 21–32, fig. 19, p. 29. The article and the exhibition in Bonn on which it is based illustrates many examples of prominent tower and high round tombs.

9 For the general type along the Rhine, see Heinz Kähler, 'Die rheinichen Pfeilergrabmäler', *Bonner Jahrbücher*, 139 (1934), pp. 145–72, and Heinz Kähler, 'Das Grabmal des L. Poblicus in Koln', *Antike Welt*, I/4 (1970), pp. 14–29; for the Publicius monument in Cologne, see Gundolf Precht, *Das Grabmal des L. Publicius* (Cologne, 1975); and for the Igel Column see Eberhard Zahn, *Die Igeler Säule bei Trier*, 4th edn (Trier, 1976), figs 10, 11.

10 H. Rolland, *Le Mausolée de Glanum (Saint-Rémy-de-Provence)*, Gallia suppl. 21 (Paris, 1969); Fred S. Kleiner, 'The Glanum Cenotaph Reliefs', *Bonner Jahrbücher*, 80 (1980), pp. 105–26; Pierre Gros, 'Le Mausolée des Julii et le Statut de Glanum', *Revue Archéologique*, 1 (1986), pp. 65–80.

11 See Alison Cooley, 'Commemorating the War Dead of the Roman World', *Proceedings of the British Academy*, CLI (2012), pp. 63–88. See also below for discussion of the Vietnam War Memorial, Washington, DC, another cenotaph.

12 Francesco Colonna, *Hypnerotomachia Poliphili: The Strife of Love in a Dream*, trans. Joscelyn Godwin (New York, 1999) with the original woodcut illustrations; fig. 13, p. 26. On the source and character of this image, see John Bury, 'Chapter III of the *Hypnerotomachia Poliphili* and the Tomb of Mausolus', *Word + Image*, XIV/1–2 (January–June 1998), pp. 40–60.

13 See especially Suzanne Glover Lindsay, 'Mummeries and Tombs: Turenne, Napoleon and Death Ritual', *Art Bulletin*, LXXXII/3 (2000), pp. 476–502.

14 See M. Raval, *Claude-Nicholas Ledoux* (Paris, 1945), pls 9–100. Ledoux was not alone in looking to Egypt and pyramidal models for tombs in France in the late eighteenth century; see Richard A. Etlin, *Symbolic Space: French Enlightenment Architecture and its Legacy* (Chicago, IL, 1994), pp. 96ff.

15 William H. Gass, 'Monumentality/Mentality', *Oppositions*, XXV (Autumn 1982), pp. 127–44, quotations pp. 129, 130, 138, 141.

16 See Drew Gilpin Faust, *This Republic of Suffering: Death and the American Civil War* (New York, 2008).

17 Reported in the *New York Times* (21 September 2014), Travel section, p. 24.

18 Gass, 'Monumentality/Mentality', pp. 131, 132.

19 Milan Kundera, *The Book of Laughter and Forgetting*, trans. M. H. Heim (New York, 1980), p. 158, on Prague; see also Gianni Vattimo, 'Post-modernity and New Monumentality', *RES*, XXVIII (1995), pp. 39–46, esp. pp. 45, 46.

20 From 'Science Times', in the *New York Times* (16 March 2010), pp. 1–4.

two

GRAVE MATTERS

1 Wilhelm Dilthey, *Das Erlebnis und die Dichtung: Lessing, Goethe, Novalis, Hölderlin*, 8th edn (Leipzig, 1922), p. 230, trans. in Joseph Koerner, *The Moment of Self-portraiture in German Renaissance Art* (Chicago, IL, 1993), p. 274.

2 For the significance of doing and saying in the conduct of life, on intention and potential narrativity, see Jerome Bruner, *Acts of Meaning* (Cambridge, MA, 1990), pp. 11–19, 33–40, 43–65, 99ff.

3 See Wolfgang Iser, *The Act of Reading: A Theory of Aesthetic Response* (Baltimore, MD, and London, 1978), pp. 118–20, 136–41, 151.

4 Maureen Carroll, *Spirits of the Dead: Roman Funerary Commemoration in Western Europe* (Oxford, 2006).

5 Richmond Lattimore, *Themes in Greek and Latin Epitaphs* (Urbana, IL, 1962).

6 Sensitively indicated by Helmut Häusle, *Das Denkmal als Garant des Nachruhms* (Munich, 1980).

7 See Roger Angell, 'Here Below', *New Yorker* (16 January 2006), pp. 38–43, quoted text on p. 38.

8 See Mireille Corbier, 'L'Écriture dans l'espace public romain', in *L'Urbs: Espace urbain et histoire* (Rome, 1987), pp. 27–60.

9 Excerpted from the translation by Jon Davies, *Death, Burial and Rebirth in the Religions of Antiquity* (New York, 1999), pp. 221–4, from the French edition of the testamentary poem, *Les Flavii du Cillium: Étude architecturale, épigraphique, historique et littéraire du mausolée de Kasserine* (Rome, 1993).

10 See Richard Sorabji, *Aristotle on Memory* (Providence, RI, 1972), pp. 47–60, translating *De memoria et reminiscentia*, §449–52; and Anita Kasabova, 'Memory, Memorials, and Commemoration', *History and Theory*, XLVII/3 (October 2008), pp. 331–50.

11 See Arthur E. Gordon, *Quintus Veranius Consul AD 49* (Berkeley and Los Angeles, CA, 1952), pp. 244–75.

12 Wilhelm Kierdorf, *Laudatio funebris: Interpretationen und Untersuchungen zur Entwicklung des römischen Leichenrede* (Meisenheim am Glan, 1980).

13 Jean Wilson, 'Lives of Quiet Usefulness in Commemoration of the Unheroic', in *Monuments for an Age without Heroes*, ed. H. Wohl and C. Velaz (Boston, MA, 1996), pp. 30–52, esp. pp. 34–5.

14 See Mark Krupnick, 'The Art of the Obituary', *American Scholar*, LXXI/4 (Autumn 2002), pp. 91–8; Anthony Lane, 'True Lives:

Preserving the Art of Writing about the Dead', *New Yorker* (27 July 1998), pp. 68–76; Mark Singer, 'The Death Beat', *New Yorker* (8 July 2002), pp. 28–32.

15 Rudyard Kipling, 'The Favour', from *Epitaphs of the War* (1914–18), at www.kiplingsociety.co.uk.

16 See István Rév, 'The Necronym', *Representations*, 64 (Autumn 1998), pp. 76–108.

17 William Hubbard, 'A Meaning for Monuments', *Public Interest*, 74 (Winter 1984), pp. 17–30; Charles L. Griswold, 'The Vietnam Veterans Memorial and the Washington Mall: Philosophical Thoughts on Political Iconography', *Critical Inquiry*, XXII/4 (Summer 1986), pp. 688–719.

18 See Peter S. Hawkins, 'Naming Names: The Art of Memory and the Names Project Aids Quilt', *Critical Inquiry*, XIX/4 (Summer 1993), pp. 752–79; Maya Lin, 'Making the Memorial', *New York Review of Books* (2 November 2000), pp. 33–5.

19 Avishai Margalit, *The Ethics of Memory* (Cambridge, MA, 2002), pp. 18–26; and Richard J. Bernstein, 'The Culture of Memory', review of Margalit's *The Ethics of Memory*, in *History and Theory*, Theme Issue 43 (December 2004), pp. 165–78.

20 On this issue see Søren Kierkegaard, *Either/Or*, Part II, ed. and trans. Howard V. Hong and Edna H. Hong (Princeton, NJ, 1984), esp. 'The Balance between the Esthetic and the Ethical in the Development of Personality', pp. 155–333.

21 Ausonius, 'Priam', from *Epitaphs of the Trojan War Heroes*, trans. Philip Massey, *Arion*, II/4 (1963), p. 60.

22 See C. P. Jones, 'An Epigram on Apollonius of Iyana', *Journal of Hellenic Studies*, 100 (1980), pp. 190–94.

23 Probably, but not certainly, Jewish. See A. Deissmann, *Light from the Ancient Past* (New York, 1927), pp. 447–50; Jean-Baptiste Frey, *Corpus Inscriptionum Iudaicarum: Europe* (Vatican City, 1936), no. 476.

24 From the *New York Times* (10 June 2014) p. A.17.

25 See Aleida Assmann, 'Texts, Traces, Trash: The Changing Media of Cultural Memory', *Representations*, 56 (Autumn 1996), pp. 123–34; Mark C. Taylor and Dietrich Christian Lammerts, *Grave Matters* (London, 2002).

26 A view of St Andrew's Church and Cemetery, located in Richmondtown, Staten Island, New York; the cemetery has been active since the early eighteenth century. From Steve Baucher and Frederick A. Winter, 'American Gravestones', *Archaeology*, XXXVI/5 (1983), pp. 46–53.

27 Jacob Grimm, *Deutsche Mythologie*, 4th edn (Berlin, 1875–8), vol. III, p. 463, no. 830.

28 For example, the Tombs of the Dons in Brooklyn and Queens which lie on consecrated ground; *New Yorker* (28 November 1977), pp. 50–53.

29 See Richard P. Saller and Brent D. Shaw, 'Tombstones and Roman Family Relations in the Principate: Civilians, Soldiers and Slaves', *Journal of Roman Studies*, LXXIV (1984), pp. 124–56; Hanne Sigismund Nielson, 'The Physical Context of Roman Epitaphs and the Structure of the Roman Family', *Analecta Romana Instituti Danici*, 23 (1996), pp. 35–60.

30 H.W.J. Drijvers, 'Ein neuentdecktes edessenisches Grabmosaik', *Antike Welt*, XII/3 (1981), pp. 17–20, fig. 1, p. 17.

31 See Ann Marie Yasin, 'Funerary Monuments and Collective Identity: From Roman Family to Christian Community', *Art Bulletin*, LXXXVII/3 (2005), pp. 433–56; Michael Koortbojian, '*In commemorationem mortuorum*: Text and Image along the "Streets of Tombs"', in *Art and Text in Roman Culture*, ed. Jaś Elsner (Cambridge, 1996), pp. 210–33, 317–26.

32 See the remarks of Antoon De Baets, 'A Declaration of the Responsibilities of Present Generations toward Past Generations', *History and Theory*, Theme Issue 43 (2004), pp. 130–64.

33 There is no question that elaborate tombs were created in the Middle Ages and early Renaissance in Western Europe, often

containing ensembles of figures in free-standing monuments,
replete with portraits and the images of saints; see Kurt Bauch,
*Das mittelalterliche Grabbild: Figürliche Grabmäler des 11. bis 15.
Jahrhunderts in Europa* (Berlin and New York, 1976). For the
flat floor tombs see Andrew Butterfield, 'Social Structure and
the Typology of Funerary Monuments in Early Renaissance
Florence', *Res*, xxvi (Autumn 1994), pp. 47–67.

34 The cenotaphic gravestone of Marcus Caelius in the
Rheinisches Landesmuseum, Bonn, has been known since the
seventeenth century; the Gallo-Roman banker and his wife
are in the Musée Bertrand in Chateauroux, near Bourges, its
base now lost; the stele of P. Longidienus, shipbuilder, is in the
Museo Nazionale di Ravenna; the so-called 'Circus Master'
is in the Musei Vaticani; for the slave trader of Amphipolis,
see H. Duchêne, 'Sur la stèle d'Aulus Caprilius Timotheos,
Somatemporis', in *Bulletin de Correspondance Hellénique*, 110
(1986), pp. 513–30; the potter and his wife are in the Virginia
Museum of Fine Arts; and for the baker's monument see
Lauren H. Petersen, 'The Baker, His Tomb, His Wife and
her Breadbasket: The Monument of Eurysaces in Rome',
Art Bulletin, lxxxv/2 (2003), pp. 230–57. For the complicated
sepulchral monument of the Haterii see Antonio Giuliano,
'Documenti per service allo studio del monumento degli
"Haterii"', *Atti dell'Accademia Nazionale dei Lincei*, Memorie
ser. viii, xiii/6 (1968), pp. 449–82, pts i–xx; William M. Jensen,
The Sculptures from the Tomb of the Haterii (Ann Arbor, mi, 1988).

35 Ursula Lange and Reiner Sörries, 'Die Procla-platte', *Antike
Welt*, xxi/1 (1990), pp. 45–56, with excellent colour illustrations,
original and reconstructed.

36 From *The Threepenny Review* (Winter 2004), an issue publishing
a 'Symposium on the Dead', pp. 26ff., photo on p. 29.

37 Photo by Tomas Munita for the *New York Times* of 28 June
2014, commemorating the Second World War and a gravesite

in Tyne Cot, Belgium, p. AI. See Jay Winter, *Sites of Memory, Sites of Mourning: The Great War in European Cultural History* (Cambridge, 1996), and the review by Thomas Laqueur, 'The Past is Past', in the *London Review of Books* (19 September 1996), pp. 3–7.

38 See James E. Young, *The Texture of Memory: Holocaust Memorials and Meanings* (New Haven, CT, 1993); Wulf Kausteiner, 'Finding Meaning in Memory: A Methodological Critique of Collective Memory Studies', *History and Theory*, 41 (May 2002), pp. 179–97.

39 See Pierre Nora's essay on the split between history and memory, in 'Between Memory and History: Les Lieux de Mémoire', *Representations*, 26 (1989), pp. 7–24.

three
MOURNING BECOMES . . .

1 See Chapter Four, and the vivid if ghastly collection of images in Paul Koudounaris, *The Empire of Death: A Cultural History of Ossuaries and Charnel Houses* (New York, 2011).

2 For example in *The Tibetan Book of the Dead*, trans. Gyurme Dorje (London, 2005), pp. 156–78; Lawrence K. Altman, 'Making the Right Call Even in Death', *New York Times* (2 July 2013), p. D3, on the accuracy of the death certificate.

3 See Midas Dekkers, *The Way of All Flesh: A Celebration of Decay* (London, 2001).

4 For the problems presented by contextual analysis and burials in a later, historical period, see John Pearce, Martin Millett and Manuela Struck, eds, *Burial Society and Context in the Roman World* (Oxford, 2000). For Prudentius' many poems on death and dying see, for example, 'That Churl Death', 'Love and Death', 'Cynthia's Illness', 'Cynthia's Near Death', 'The Death of Marcellus', 'Cynthia's Ghost', in A. G. Watts, ed.,

The Poems of Prudentius (Baltimore, MD, 1966), pp. 61, 107, 108, 153, 184.

5 Prudentius, 'Burial of the Dead', from Helen Waddell, *The Wandering Scholars* (New York, 1955), p. 20.

6 Bronisław Malinomski, *Magic, Science and Religion*, 2nd edn (New York, 1954), pp. 47–48, 50, cited in Keith Hopkins, *Death and Renewal* (Cambridge, 1983), p. 224.

7 Hopkins, *Death and Renewal*, pp. 217–35; S. P. Scott, 'The Laws of the Twelve Tables', *The Civil Law*, vol. I, Laws vii–ix, xiv–xviii; Kaufmann Kohler, 'Burial', in *Jewish Encyclopedia*, vol. III (New York, 1903), pp. 432–7; Leon Halevi, *Muhammad's Grave: Death Rites and the Making of Islamic Society* (New York, 2011), pp. 43–142.

8 Susan Sontag, 'Nádas's Comedy of Interment', *Common Knowledge*, VIII/1 (2002). The play is on pp. 218–68, trans. Imre Goldstein.

9 Wallace Stevens, 'Like Decorations in a Nigger Cemetery', written for his friend Arthur Powell, in *Poems: Wallace Stevens*, ed. Samuel French Morse (New York, 1959), p. 60.

10 Jacques Derrida, *The Work of Mourning*, ed. Pascale-Anne Brault and Michael Naas (Chicago, IL, 2001); on his memoir of Louis Marion see p. 159, and 'Introduction', pp. 8–10. See also Derrida, 'By Force of Mourning', *Critical Inquiry*, XXII/2 (Winter 1996), pp. 171–92, and Derrida, 'Adieu', *Critical Inquiry*, XXIII/1 (Autumn 1996), pp. 1–10, both translated by Brault and Naas.

11 From Sherene Baugher and Frederick A. Winter, 'Early American Gravestones', *Archaeology*, XXXVI/5 (September–October 1983), pp. 47–54. Note, the words 'In God We Trust' also appear on U.S. currency, and whether they suggest Clark's economic views or not is uncertain.

12 Responses to this situation are many, but see two recent studies that offer guidance: Thomas Attig, *How We Grieve: Relearning the World* (Oxford, 1996), based on real-life stories;

and George A. Bonanno, *The Other Side of Sadness: What the New Science of Bereavement Tells Us about Life After Loss* (New York, 2009), which emphasizes resiliency.

13 Thomas H. Johnson, *The Complete Poems of Emily Dickinson* (Boston, MA, and Toronto, 1960), no. 360, pp. 170–71, *c.* 1862.

14 Paul Celan, *Poems of Paul Celan*, trans. Michael Hamburger (New York, 1995), pp. 63, 64; see also John Simon, 'Death Fugues: The Poems of Paul Celan', *New Criterion* (May 1996), pp. 28–38.

15 Helen Rappaport, *Magnificent Obsession: Victoria, Albert and the Death that Changed the Monarchy* (London, 2011); Albert died in late 1861.

16 See Drew Gilpin Faust, *This Republic of Suffering: Death and the American Civil War* (New York, 2008); Mark Sanchez, *Awaiting the Heavenly Country: The Civil War and America's Culture of Death* (Ithaca, NY, 2008).

17 See Sandra W. Gilbert, *Death's Door: Modern Dying and the Ways We Grieve* (New York, 2005), for an extended analysis of the realities of mourning.

18 William Carlos Williams, *Selected Poems* (New York, 1949), p. 25; see also Theocritus, 'The Lament for Adonis', *Idylls*, written in the third century BCE in Hellenistic Alexandria, imagined but no less poignant; Ovid, *Metamorphoses*, Book x, ll. 821–57.

19 Quoting from the tenth-century Andalusian poet Ibn Abi-Zamanin, Richard Covington on the exhibition 'Roads of Arabia', *Aramco World* (March–April 2011), p. 35.

20 Marcus Cornelius Fronto, 'My Lord M. Aurelius Antonius', trans. Philip Murray, in *Arion*, II/2 (1963), p. 28, reprinted from *Hudson Review*, xv/4 (Winter 1962–3).

21 *The Nation* (29 October 2001); written as a form of elegy.

22 After Pat Conway, 'Losses and Grief in Old Age', *Social Casework*, LXIX/9 (1988), pp. 541–55.

23 See Joan Melville, 'Inventions of Farewell'; Wallace Stevens's 'The Owl in the Sarcophagus', *Wallace Stevens Journal*, 164 (1992), pp. 3–21, for the later poem. 'A Clear Day and No Memories', in *Poems: Wallace Stevens*, p. 168.

24 For example see David Rieff, *Swimming a Sea of Death: A Son's Memoir* (New York, 2008); Julian Barnes, *Levels of Life* (New York, 2013); David Grossman, *Falling Out of Time* (New York, 2014); Alec Wilkinson, 'Finding the Words . . . the Poet Edward Hirsch Imparts the Loss of his Son', *New Yorker* (4 August 2014), pp. 48–57.

25 Barbara J. King, *How Animals Grieve* (Chicago, IL, 2013). Communal grieving is especially strong among elephants, because of the close relation among members of the herd and with the herd's matriarch.

26 On the alleged resilience of survivors see Bonanno, *The Other Side of Sadness*, pp. 45–94.

27 From John H. Taylor, *Journey through the Afterlife: Ancient Egyptian Book of the Dead* (Cambridge, MA, 2010), pp. 94, 95, from the Papyrus of Hunefer, 19th dynasty.

28 See Erwin Panofsky, *Tomb Sculpture: Its Changing Aspects from Ancient Egypt to Bernini* (New York, 1964).

29 On the elegiac nature of this composition see Gregory Orn, 'Praxiteles and the Shapes of Grief', *New Literary History*, 37 (2006), pp. 673–80.

30 Heinrich Heine, 'Memorial Service', in 'From the Mattress Grave: 3 Late Poems by Heinrich Heine', trans. Martin Greenberg, *New Criterion* (March 1993), p. 49 (the last four stanzas are omitted here).

31 See David Carrier, 'Circa 1640', *New Literary History*, XXI/3 (1990), pp. 649–70, reinterpreting Panofsky's interpretation of Poussin's *The Arcadian Shepherds* and the phrase '*et in Arcadia ego*'.

32 On this important point see the contribution in 'A Symposium on the Dead' in *The Threepenny Review* (Winter 2004), pp. 26–31.

four

THE REMAINS

1 Brian Copenhaver, *Hermetica: The Greek Corpus Hermeticum and the Latin Asclepius in a New English Translation, with Notes and Introduction* (Cambridge, 1998), Hermetica XI.15, p. 40.

2 Wendy Cope, 'Once I'm Dead', *TLS* (15 October 2010), www.the-tls.co.uk.

3 Epicurus, *Key Doctrines* 2 and the *Letter to Menoeceus*, sections 124, 125; see James Warren, *Facing Death: Epicurus and His Critics* (Oxford, 2004), and Julian Barnes, *Nothing to Be Frightened Of* (New York, 2008).

4 After Richard Sorabji, *Self: Ancient and Modern Thoughts about Individuality, Life, and Death* (Chicago, IL, 2006), esp. pp. 94–111, 301–15.

5 As reported in the *New York Times* (23 March 2015), p. A4, and other newspapers in the United States and Britain.

6 *New York Times* (16 March 2015), p. C6.

7 Anne Carson, *Yale Journal of Criticism*, VI/1 (1993), pp. 75–92; see also Lawrence Stone, 'Death and its History', *New York Review of Books* (12 October 1978), pp. 22–30; Timothy Taylor, *The Buried Soul: How Humans Invented Death* (Boston, MA, 2004).

8 Sotheby's, New York, *Antiquities* (10 December 2009), no. 42, p. 44; Friedrich Matz, *Die dionysische Sarkophage*, vol. XLIV (Berlin, 1975), pp. 467, 469–70, no. 278, pl. 3031; Robert Turcan, *Les Sarcophages romains à représentations dionysiaques* (Paris, 1966), pp. 80, 81, 543.

9 See Willibald Sauerländer, 'Germany: When Faces Defied Death', *New York Review of Books* (24 November 2011), pp. 61–3, reviewing the rise of portraiture revealed in an exhibition in Vienna and Munich, 2011–12, entitled 'The Discovery of Man: German Portraiture around 1500'.

10 Following the excellent article '"Holy Trinity" by Mosaccio: A Convergence of Faith and Reason' by Jack Flam in the *Wall Street Journal* (18–19 February 2012), p. c13.

11 After Terry Eagleton's review of Douglas Turner, *Thomas Aquinas: A Portrait* (New Haven, CT, 2013), in the *London Review of Books* (5 December 2013), p. 39.

12 See *The Art Newspaper*, 244 (March 2013), p. 5, with this illustration.

13 See Francis Robicsek, *The Maya Book of the Dead: The Ceramic Codex* (Charlottesville, VA, 1981), pp. 56, 62, Vessel 65.

14 See for example Ann Fabian, *The Skull Collectors* (Chicago, IL, 2012).

15 Damien Hirst, 'The Skull Beneath the Skin', from the series *New Religion* (2005).

16 See Bernard Andreae, 'Vita e morte. Figure umana in alcuni mosaici antichi', *Forma Urbis*, 11 (November 2002), pp. 121–36.

17 Mechthild Haas, ed., *Art in Transition: Albrecht Dürer* (Washington, DC, 2008), cat. no. 78, pp. 108–9.

18 Still in the spirit of Thomas Adès's *Totentanz*, a vocal-orchestral work premiered in New York in March 2015.

19 For William Combe, *The English Dance of Death* and *The English Dance of Life* (London, 1814–17); see the Swann advertisement in the *New Yorker* (1 April 2013), p. 11, which has a long record of cartoons joking about death, as in the series 'Grin and Bear It', *New Yorker* (31 October 2011), pp. 72–3.

20 Lairesse's illustrations were also used in William Cowper's sumptuous edition *The Anatomy of Human Bodies* (Leiden, 1737).

21 See Joseph Leo Koerner, 'The Mortification of the Image: Death as a Hermeneutic in Hans Baldung Grien', in *Representations*, 10 (Spring 1985), pp. 52–100, illustration fig. 10, p. 79; also Georges Bataille, *Eroticism: Death and Sensuality*, trans. Mary Dalwood (San Francisco, CA, 1986), pp. 55–108, pl. iv.

22 Robert Crumb, *The Book of Genesis Illustrated* (New York and London, 2009), illustrations in ch. 3 (unpaginated).

23 Hogarth's painting is now in the Tate Gallery, London, and follows Milton's poem very closely; see Howard J. M. Hanley, 'Satin, Sin and Death', *Apollo* (August 1998), pp. 35–40, fig. 1, p. 35.

24 Candace Black, ed., *Sade, Sex and Death: The Divine Marquis and the Surrealists*, trans. R. J. Dent (Los Angeles, CA, 2011).

25 Wallace Stevens, 'A Clear Day and No Memories', in *Poems: Wallace Stevens* (New York, 1959), p. 168; see also Geoff Archer, *The Glorious Dead: Figurative Sculpture of British First World War Memorials* (Norwich, 2009), with allegorical motifs of Peace, Victory, Death and Eternal Sleep.

26 Hazel Dodge, 'Amusing the Masses', in D. S. Potter and D. J. Mattingly, *Life, Death and Entertainment in the Roman Empire* (Ann Arbor, MI, 1999), pp. 205–99; David S. Potter, 'Entertainment in the Roman Empire', ibid., pp. 303–25; Tertullian, *De spectaculis*, trans. T. R. Glover (Cambridge, 1931), xii–xxi, pp. 263–83; Caroline A. Barton, 'The Scandal of the Arena', *Representations*, 27 (1989), pp. 1–36.

27 Jee Lee Hong, 'Theatricalizing Death and Society in *The Skeletons' Illusory Performance* by Li Song', *Art Bulletin*, XVIII/1 (2011), pp. 60–78, fig. 1, p. 61.

28 See also Chapter Five.

29 See the cover of R. Andrew Chesnut, *Devoted to Death: Santa Muerte, the Skeleton Saint* (Oxford, 2012).

30 See Karina Croucher, *Death and Dying in the Neolithic Near East* (Oxford, 2012); Denise Schmandt-Besserat, 'Stone Age Death Masks', *Archaeology Odyssey* (March–April 2003).

31 See Paul Koudounaris, *Heavenly Body: Cult Treasures and Spectacular Saints from the Catacombs* (London, 2013), and Marcia Pointon, 'Casts, Imprints, and the Deathliness of Things: Artifacts on the Edge', *Art Bulletin*, XCVI/2 (2014), pp. 156–95, with many illustrations.

32 With the exception of Jeremy Bentham's auto-icon (1836) in University College London.

33 Allen Ginsberg, 'Complaint of the Skeleton to Time', in *Collected Poems, 1947–1980* (New York, 1984), p. 17.

34 See Paul Plass, *The Game of Death in Ancient Rome* (Madison, WI, 1995); Donald G. Kyle, *Spectacles of Death in Ancient Rome* (London, 1998); K. M. Coleman, 'Fatal Charades: Roman Executions Staged as Mythological Enactments', *Journal of Roman Studies*, LXXX (1990), pp. 44–71.

35 Bibliothèque Nationale, Paris, Ms. Lat. 9471, f. 135, from E. Panofsky, *Tomb Sculptures*, fig. 72; see also Ashby Kinch, *Imago Mortis: Mediating Images of Death in Late Medieval Culture* (Boston, MA, and Leiden, 2013); and Caroline Bruzelius, *Preaching, Building, and Burying: Friars in the Medieval City* (New Haven, CT, 2015), on the role of the mendicant orders in Siena, Naples and Florence.

36 After Julia Kristeva, 'Holbein's Dead Christ', in *Zone 3: Fragments of the History of the Human Body, Part 1*, ed. Michel Feher, Ramona Naddaff and Nadia Tazi (New York, 1989), pp. 238–69, fig. on pp. 238–9; note that according to St Augustine, the death of the body is man's peculiar punishment, in his *The Enchiridion: On Faith, Hope and Love*, XXV, trans. J. F. Shaw, ed. Henry Paolucci (Chicago, IL, 1961), p. 31.

37 See Judith Shulevitz, 'Is This a Corpse Which I See Before Me? How Science is Changing What it Means to be Dead', *New Republic*, CCXLV/13 (4 August 2014), p. 7.

38 Diana Fuss, 'Corpse Poem', *Critical Inquiry*, XXX/1 (Autumn 2003), pp. 1–30.

39 Emily Dickinson, *The Poems of Emily Dickinson*, ed. R. W. Franklin (Cambridge, MA, 1998), p. 1027.

40 See for example Douglas Preston, 'The 9,000-year-old Man Speaks', Smithsonian.com, September 2014; Jennifer Couzin-Frankel, 'Divulging DNA Secrets of Dead Stirs

Debate', *Science*, CCCXLIII/6169 (24 January 2014), pp. 356–7;
Glenn Hodges, 'The First Face of the First Americans Belongs
to an Unlucky Teenage Girl', *National Geographic* (January
2015), pp. 125–37; she died 12–13,000 years ago.

41 The reconstructed head is illustrated in Preston, 'The 9,000-
year-old Man Speaks'.

42 But see also Audrey Linkman, *Photography and Death* (London,
2011), which is not concerned with images of death caused by
war, violence or natural disasters but instead concentrates on
the peaceful, quiet images of relatives and friends.

43 Death rituals vary enormously from culture to culture, but many
have common features; for a general perspective see Philippe
Ariès, *The Hour of Our Death* (New York, 1981); Leon Halavi's
Muhammad's Grave: Death Rites and the Making of Islamic Society
(New York, 2007); Sinan Antoon, *The Corpse Washer* (New Haven,
CT, 2014); and *The Tibetan Book of the Dead*, trans. Gyurme Dorje
(London, 2005), on the signs of death, pp. 155–95.

44 *New York Times* (22 June 2014), pp. 1–14.

45 Yoel Hoffmann, ed. and trans., *Japanese Death Poems* (Boston,
MA, 1986), p. 107.

46 David Wagoner, 'A Congo Funeral', in *The American Scholar*,
LXXIII/4 (2004), p. 60.

47 See the poem 'At the End of Life, a Secret' by Reginald
Dwayne Betts, in *Poetry*, CCI/2 (November 2012), p. 149.

48 The problem is well discussed by Marcia Angell in 'May
Doctors Help You to Die?', *New York Review of Books*
(11 October 2012), pp. 39–42, and 'How to Die in Massachusetts',
New York Review of Books (21 February 2013), pp. 27–8.

49 See Norman Cantor, *After We Die: The Life and Times of the
Human Cadaver* (New York, 2010), on the perils of cremation
inter alia.

50 See Michael Ignatieff, 'After Hell: Life in the Ashes of World
War II', *New Republic* (30 June 2014), pp. 48–51, photograph p. 48.

five

ON THE VERGE OF DEATH

1 After the model of the cultural significance of keywords in Raymond Williams, *Keywords: A Vocabulary of Culture and Society*, revd edn (Oxford, 2015).

2 Agatha Christie, 'Hercule Poirot is Agatha Christie's *Chef-d'Oeuvre*', in the first edition of Christie's *Appointment with Death* (London, 1938).

3 On this point, see Maristella de Panizza Lorch, '*Mors Omnia Vincit Improba*: l'uomo e la morte nel *De Voluptate – De vero falso que bono di Lorenzo Valla* (II., Cap. XXIX)', in *Umanesimo e rinascimento a Firenze e a Venezia, Misc. di Studi in onore di Vittore Branca*, vol. III (Florence, 1983), pp. 177–92.

4 For the Policoro vase, fourth century BCE, see the *Illustrated London News* (16 September 1967), p. 29; for the Farnese Bull and its complicated history see Francis Haskell and Nicholas Penny, *Taste and the Antique* (New Haven, CT, 1981), no. 13, pp. 165–7, fig. 85.

5 See John Peter Oleson, 'Greek Myth and Etruscan Imagery in the Tomb of the Bulls at Tarquinia', *American Journal of Archaeology*, LXXIX/3 (1975), pp. 189–200, pls 35–7.

6 Simon A. Grolnick and Alfonz Lengyel, 'Etruscan Burial Symbols and the Transitional Process', in *Between Reality and Fantasy: Transitional Objects and Phenomena*, ed. Simon A. Grolnick and Leonard Buskin (New York, 1978), pp. 381–410.

7 Richard Brilliant, *Visual Narratives* (Ithaca, NY, 1984), pp. 126–32.

8 Petrarch, *Rime Sparse*, 23.147–60, in Robert M. Durling, ed., *Petrarch's Lyric Poems* (Cambridge, MA, 1967), p. 67.

9 See for example James Goodman, *But Where is the Lamb? Imagining the Story of Abraham and Isaac* (New York, 2014)

and Jeremy Wanderer, 'Silence of the Lambs', *Jewish Review of Books* (Winter 2015), pp. 14–16.

10 On the painting of Daniel, see Joseph Vogt, 'Christenverfolgungen in antiken Rome', *Antike Welt*, VII/4 (1976), pp. 48–59, fig. 10, p. 56; for the Vatican sarcophagus, see Friedrich W. Deichmann, *Repertorium der christlich-antiken Sarkophage*, vol. 1: *Rome und Ostia* (Wiesbaden, 1967), no. 44, pl. 14.

11 Antonio Ferrua, *The Unknown Catacomb* (Florence, 1990; Eng. edn 1991), cubiculum N, pp. 130–41, fig. 128, p. 137; see also fig. v.7, the Sacrifice of Isaac from the same catacomb, ibid., fig. 68, p. 91; see also Susan Wood, 'Alcestis on Roman Sarcophagi', *American Journal of Archaeology*, 82 (1978), pp. 499–510, and Charles Segal, 'Cold Delight: Art, Death, and the Transgression of Genre in Euripides' *Alcestis*', in *The Scope of Words: In Honor of Albert S. Cook*, ed. Peter Baker et al. (New York, 1991), pp. 211–28.

12 Gottfried Benn, 'Death of Orpheus' (1940–50), trans. Michael Hofmann, *Times Literary Supplement* (9 October 2009), p. 12; Rainer Maria Rilke, *Sonnets to Orpheus*, II.13, trans. Stephen Mitchell in *Selected Poetry of Rainer Maria Rilke* (New York, 1982); Czesław Miłosz, 'Orpheus and Eurydice' (2002), in *Second Space: New Poems by Czeslaw Milosz* (New York, 2004); and Louise Glück, 'Relic' (1999). Most of these were included in a musical performance of Glück's poetry at Tanglewood, Massachusetts, in July 2008.

13 Louise Gluck's *Averno* was performed as the text of a cantata by the same name written by Elena Ruehr and performed by the Trinity Choir, Trinity Church, New York City, 19 May 2011.

14 See Emeline Richardson, 'The Story of Ariadne in Italy', in *Studies in Classical Art and Archaeology*, ed. G. Kopcke and Mary B. Moore (New York, 1979), pp. 189–95, pls LII–LIV.

15 After Paul Zanker and Björn Christian Ewald, *Mit Mythen Leben: Die Bilderwelt des römischer Sarkophage* (Munich, 2004), pp. 135ff., 162–7; see the informative review by Christopher H. Hallett, *Art Bulletin*, 871 (2005), pp. 157–61.

16 Marion Lawrence, 'The Velletri Sarcophagus', *American Journal of Archaeology*, 69 (1965), pp. 207–22; B. Andreae, *Studien zur römischen Grabkunst* (Heidelberg, 1963), pp. 11–87; Zanker and Ewald, *Mit Mythen Leben*, fig. 21, p. 30.

17 On the importance of keeping separate these distinct realities, see Plotinus, *Ennead*, III.5.24–9.

18 Britt Haarløv, *The Half-open Door: A Common Symbolic Motif within Roman Sepulchral Sculpture* (Odense, 1977), reviewed by Jan Białostocki in *Art Bulletin*, LXI/2 (1979), pp. 301, 302.

19 Pausanias, *The Itinerary of Greece*, 10.4.4; Horace, *Carmina*, 1.16.13–16.

20 Hesiod, *Theogony*, 506–616; Aeschylus, *Prometheus Unbound*.

21 Moreau's painting in the Musée Gustave Moreau, Paris, depicts a vulture eating Prometheus' liver, rather than the canonical eagle; G. Lacambre, *Gustave Moreau* (Paris, 1999), no. 37, pp. 106–8; for the eschatological, political and psychoanalytic conception of Prometheus' role in literature and art, see C. Kerényi, *Prometheus: Archetypal Image of Human Existence* (London, 1963).

22 Lucretius, *De rerum natura*, 3.870–83, quoted in James Warren, *Facing Death: Epicurus and his Critics* (Oxford, 2004), p. 21.

23 Thomas Hobbes, *Leviathan*, 12.5.

24 See for example Victoria C. Gardner Coates, Kenneth Lapatin and Jon L. Seydl, *The Last Days of Pompeii* (Los Angeles, CA, and Cleveland, OH, 2012), p. 27.

25 Roland Barthes, *Camera Lucida: Reflections in Photography*, trans. Richard Howard (New York, 1981), p. 92; note the commentary by Peter Schwenger, 'Corpsing the Image', *Critical Inquiry*, XXVI/3 (2000), pp. 395–413.

26 David Hume, *Essays Moral, Political, and Literary*, ed. Eugene F. Miller (Indianapolis, IN, 1985), pp. 585, 586.

27 From Kathryn Schulz, 'Final Forms: What Death Certificates Can Tell Us and What They Can't', *New Yorker* (7 April 2014), pp. 32–7. See also Walter Hadwen et al., *Premature Burial* (London, 2013), on the perils of when the determination of death was uncertain and people worried about being buried alive.

28 Angie Estes, 'How to Know When the Dead are Dead', in *American Scholar* (Autumn 2012), p. 57.

29 See especially Atul Gawande, *Being Mortal: Medicine and What Matters in the End* (New York, 2014).

30 On the 'legacy video' see the *Wall Street Journal* (4 February 2014), p. DI, and on the 'farewell party' see the *New York Times* (14 January 2014), p. A20.

31 See L. W. Sumner, *Assisted Death: A Study in Ethics and Law* (Oxford, 2011), and the review by Thomas Nagel with the title 'In Whose Interest', *London Review of Books* (6 October 2011), pp. 13, 14.

32 Kathleen M. Coleman, 'Fatal Charades', *Journal of Roman Studies*, LXXX (1990), pp. 44–73.

33 See Susan Gubar, 'In the Chemo Colony', *Critical Inquiry*, XXXVII/4 (2011), pp. 652–70; compare the contrasting attitudes of the Michigan Commission on Death and Dying, viewed as 'An Opportunity Lost' by Joseph Ellin, *Journal of Sociology and Social Welfare*, XXII/3 (1995), pp. 3–24; and the Supreme Court of New Jersey, 'In the Matter of Kathleen Farrell', *New Jersey Reports*, 108 (1988), pp. 335–65.

34 The argument expressed by Jennifer Worth, *In the Midst of Life* (London, 2011).

six

AFTER ALL, WE DIE, AND THEN?

1 Seneca, *Seneca: 17 Letters*, trans. C.D.N. Costa (Warminster, 1998), pp. 23–7; see Catharine Edwards, *Death in Ancient Rome* (New Haven, CT, 2007), pp. 78–112.

2 Barry Goldensohn, 'Remains', *New Republic* (18 August 2011), p. 30.

3 The slogan 'food for vultures' is taken from Rami Arav, 'Excarnation: Food for Vultures', in *Biblical Archaeology Review* (November–December 2011), pp. 40–49; see also James Mellaart, *Çatal Hüyük: A Neolithic Town in Anatolia* (New York, 1967).

4 *New York Times* (30 November 2012), p. A18.

5 Diana Fuss, 'Corpse Poem', *Critical Inquiry*, XXX (2003), pp. 1–30, with several examples; see also Mark Johnston, *Surviving Death* (Princeton, NJ, 2014), ch. 5, 'A New Refutation of Death', on the role of the continuum 'I' as an instrument of the afterlife.

6 A. E. Watts, trans. and ed., *The Poems of Propertius* (Baltimore, MD, 1961), IV.vii, 'Cynthia's Ghost', pp. 184–7.

7 Michael Longley, 'The Apparition', *TLS* (27 September 2013), p. 9; the poem is dedicated 'for Peter, my twin'.

8 Virgil, *Aeneid*, II.270ff.

9 *Vatican Virgil*, Vat. Lat. 3225, f.19v., in David H. Wright, *The Vatican Virgil: A Masterpiece of Late Antique Art* (Berkeley and Los Angeles, CA, 1993), fig. 15, p. 127; see the excellent, vivid translation by Robert Fagles, *Virgil: The Aeneid* (New York, 2006), pp. 84ff.

10 See Hans Belting, 'Aus dem Schatten des Todes. Bild und Körper un den Anfängen', in *Der Tod in den Weltkulturen und Weltreligionen*, ed. C. von Barloewen (Munich, 1995), pp. 92–136.

11 *Biblical Archaeology Review* (July–August 2011), p. 72; Dennis Pardee, 'The Katumuwa Inscription', in *In Remembrance of Me: Feasting with the Dead in the Ancient Middle East*, ed. Virginia

Rimmer Herrmann and J. David Schloen (Chicago, IL, 2014), p. 45.

12 See Leslee Goodman, 'Between Two Worlds: Malidoma Somé on Rites of Passage', *Sun Magazine* (July 2010), pp. 5–11, on the vital importance of the relationship between ancestors and descendants to maintain the spirits of the dead; also Malidoma Somé, a native of Burkina Faso, on the destructive effects of hostile cultural intrusions in *Ritual: Power, Healing, and Community* (New York, 1997).

13 Pliny the Elder, *Natural History*, VII.188.

14 See the arguments presented for the prevalence of collective memory, and afterlife, by Samuel Scheffler, *Death and the Afterlife* (Oxford, 2014).

15 See the reviews of Scheffler's book by Thomas Nagel in the *New York Review of Books* (9 January 2014), pp. 26–8; Amia Srinivasan in the *London Review of Books* (25 September 2014), pp. 13–14; and David Owens in the *TLS* (21 February 2014), pp. 21–2.

16 Ovid, *Metamorphoses*, Book 6.

17 Mario Napoli, *La Tomba del tuffatore* (Bari, 1970); Agnès Rouveret, 'La peinture dans l'art funéraire: La Tombe du Plongeur à Paestum', in *Recherches pour les religions de l'Italie antique*, vol. VII, ed. Raymond Bloch (Paris, 1976), pp. 99–129.

18 See earlier chapters; note Mary-Ann Pouls Wegner, 'Gateway to the Netherworld', on Abydos, Egypt, in *Archaeology* (January–February 2013), pp. 50–53; M. A. Elferink, *La Descente de l'âme d'après Macrobe* (Leiden, 1968), on Macrobius' Neoplatonic view of the soul.

19 Moshe Barasch, 'The Departing Soul: The Long Life of a Medieval Creation', *Artibus et Historiae*, 52 (2009), pp. 13–28. Apotheosis and resurrection are discussed later in this chapter.

20 See the very useful, well-illustrated guide to the paintings by Dugald McLellan, *Guida agli affreschi di Luca Signorelli nella*

cappella Nuova o di San Brizio del Duomo di Orvieto (Orvieto, 1998); in general, Tom Henry, *The Art and Life of Luca Signorelli* (New Haven, CT, 2012).

21 Ghisi's engraving is after a mid-sixteenth-century painting by Giovanni Battista Bertini; see Paolo Bellini, ed., *L'opera incisa di Giorgio Ghisi* (Bassano del Grappa, 1998), pp. 112–14; on other precedents see Claude Bérard, *Anodoi: Essai sur l'imagerie des passages chthoniens*, Biblioteca Helvetica Romana XIII (Berne, 1974), pl. 20, pp. 146, 166f.

22 Wallace Stevens, 'As You Leave the Room', in *Poems: Wallace Stevens* (New York, 1959), p. 168.

23 See Eleanor Heartney on the work of Sally Mann, in 'The Forensic Eye', *Art in America* (January 2005), pp. 50–55, on Mann's photographs of death and decay.

24 From the Joan and Victor Johnson Collection in Meadowbrook near Philadelphia; see Lisa Minardi, 'Drawn with Spirit: Pennsylvania German Fraktur', *Antique and Fine Art*, 15th Anniversary, 1015 (2015), pp. 138–47, illus. p. 145; see also Anthony Kelly, *Eschatology and Hope* (Maryknoll, NY, 2008), on when death occurs as a moment of truth about one's life.

25 David Grosmann, *Falling Out of Time* (New York, 2014), p. 192.

26 Presence and absence seem part of Mark Johnston's thinking in his book *Surviving Death* (Princeton, NJ, 2010).

27 See Louisa Buck, 'Ed Atkins, Vile and Virtual Bodies', *The Art Newspaper*, 258 (June 2014), pp. 65–6; David Segal, 'This Man is Not a Cyborg. Yet', *New York Times* (2 June 2013), Sunday Business, pp. 1, 4, 5.

28 See Fernando Vidal, 'Brains, Bodies, Selves, and Science: Anthropologies of Identity and the Resurrection of the Body', *Critical Inquiry*, XXVIII (2002), pp. 930–74; see 'One Death Provides New Life for Many', *New York Times* (17 May 2011), Science Times, pp. 1, 6.

29 See Susan Wood, 'Mortals, Empresses, and Earth Goddesses – Demeter and Persephone in Public and Private Apotheosi', in *I Claudia II: Women in Roman Art and Society*, ed. Diana E. E. Kleiner and Susan B. Matheson (Austin, TX, 2001), pp. 77–99.

30 Archer St Clair, 'The Apotheosis Diptych', *Art Bulletin*, XLVI/4 (1964), fig. 1, pp. 205–24; deified emperors do not die, see Elias Bickerman, 'Consecratio', *Le Culte des souverains dans l'Empire romain* (Geneva, 1973), pp. 3–25; Simon Price, 'From Noble Funerals to Divine Cult: The Consecration of Roman Emperors', in *Rituals of Royalty: Power and Ceremonial in Traditional Societies*, ed. D. Cannadine and S. Price (Cambridge, 1987), pp. 56–105.

31 On the problematic concept of personal identity first articulated by John Locke, *Essay Concerning Human Understanding*, Book Two, ch. 27, see Galen Strawson, *Locke on Personal Identity* (Princeton, NJ, 2012).

32 See Ian Morris, *Death: Ritual and Social Structure in Classical Antiquity* (Cambridge, 1952), pp. 31–69.

33 Cicero, *De Republica*, XI.14.

34 Athenagoras, late second-century Christian author of a *Treatise on the Resurrection of the Dead: De Resurrectione*, section 7; see Leslie Barnard, 'Notes on Athenagoras', *Latomus*, XXXI/2 (1972), pp. 413–32, quotation p. 426.

35 Pliny the Elder, *Natural History*, VII.188.

36 The theme of Peter Brown's recent book *The Ransom of the Soul: Afterlife and Wealth in Early Christianity* (Cambridge, MA, 2015), and the excellent review by C. W. Bowersock, 'Memory and Your Soul', *New York Review of Books* (21 May 2015), pp. 28–30.

37 See Elizabeth Struthers Malbon, *The Iconography of the Sarcophagus of Junior Bassus Neofitus Sit Ad Deum* (Princeton, NJ, 1990).

38 See M. Bagnoli, H. Klein et al., eds, *Treasures of Heaven: Saints, Relics, and Devotion in Medieval Europe*, exh. cat., Walters Art

Museum, Baltimore, MD (2010), pp. 18–28, 54–67; and Robert Bartlett, *Why Can the Dead Do Such Great Things? Saints and Worshippers from the Martyrs to the Reformation* (Princeton, NJ, 2013), ch. 8, 'Relics and Shrines', pp. 239–332.

39 Charles Freeman, *Holy Bones, Holy Dust: How Relics Shaped the History of Medieval Europe* (New Haven, CT, 2011): Caroline Wallace Bynum, *Christian Materiality: An Essay on Religion in Late Medieval Europe* (New York, 2011).

40 Maximus of Tyre, *The Philosophical Orations*, trans. M. B. Trapp (Oxford, 1997), oration 10, pp. 85, 88.

41 Todd Burgo with Lynn Vincent, *Heaven is for Real: A Little Boy's Astounding Story of a Trip to Heaven and Back* (Nashville, TN, 2010); see Robert Gottlieb, 'To Heaven and Back', *New York Review of Books* (23 October 2014), pp. 75–7, with a list of related books on p. 75, the titles of some given here: *Heaven is for Real: A Little Boy's Astounding Story of His Trip to Heaven and Back*; *Life After Life: The Investigation of a Phenomenon – Survival of Bodily Death*; *Paranormal: My Life in Pursuit of the Afterlife*; *Evidence of the Afterlife: The Science of Near-death Experiences*; and *Proof of Heaven: A Neurosurgeon's Journey into the Afterlife*.

42 Oliver Sacks, *Hallucinations* (New York, 2012); Burkhard Bilger, 'The Possibilities', *New Yorker* (25 April 2011), pp. 54–65.

43 *London Review of Books* (14 April 2015), pp. 3–9, quotation on p. 3.

44 John Casey, *After Lives* (Oxford, 2010), pp. 245–355.

45 See Jacques Derrida, 'White Mythology: Metaphor in the Text of Philosophy', *New Literary History*, VI/1 (1974), pp. 5–74; the essay originally appeared as 'La Mythologie blanche', *Poétique*, 5 (1971), and has been translated here by F.C.T. Moore.

46 See Norman Cantor, *After We Die: The Life and Times of the Human Cadaver* (Georgetown, WA, 2011).

47 After Jeffrey P. Bishop, *The Anticipatory Corpse* (Indianapolis, IN, 2011), pp. 14–16.

48 Scheffler, *Death and the Afterlife*, esp. pp. 75–81; Seamus Heaney, *Human Chain* (New York, 2010), for whom 'the dead here are borne towards the future'.

49 See Dick Teresi, *The Undead* (New York, 2012), esp. 'The Brain Death Revolution', pp. 89–140, and 'The New Undead', pp. 141–69.

50 See Abigail Tucker, 'The Great New England Vampire Panic', Smithsonian.com, October 2012.

51 Martin Heidegger, *Being and Time*, trans. John Macquarrie and Edward Robinson, from the 7th edn of *Sein und Zeit* (New York, 1962), pp. 278–311.

52 Graham John Pollard, *Renaissance Medals: National Gallery of Art* (New York and Oxford, 2005), vol. III, pp. 767–8. Erasmus' motto should be compared with John Keats, who knew he was dying of consumption at age 25; see Stanley Plumly, *Posthumous Keats: A Personal Biography* (New York, 2009).

53 Brian Copenhaver, *Hermetics: The Greek Corpus Hermeticum and the Latin Asclepius in a New English Translation, with Notes and Introduction* (Cambridge, 1998), Hermetica XI.15, p. 40.

Select Bibliography

Barnes, Julian, *Nothing to Be Frightened Of* (New York, 2008)

Bishop, Jeffrey P., *The Anticipatory Corpse: Medicine, Power, and the Care of the Dying* (Notre Dame, IN, 2011)

Casey, John, *After Lives: A Guide to Heaven, Hell, and Purgatory* (Oxford, 2009)

Chesnut, R. Andrew, *Devoted to Death: Santa Muerte, the Skeleton Saint* (Oxford, 2012)

Davies, John, *Death, Burial and Rebirth in the Religions of Antiquity* (London and New York, 1999)

Derrida, Jacques, *The Gift of Death* 2nd edition and *Literature in Secret*, trans. David Wills (Chicago, IL, 2008)

Ferrarotti, Franco, *Vietato morire* (Imola, 2004)

Gray, John, *The Immortalization Commission: Science and the Strange Quest to Cheat Death* (New York, 2011)

Gutkind, Lee, *At the End of Life: True Stories about How We Die* (Pittsburgh, PA, 2011)

Halevi, Leor, *Muhammad's Grave: Death Rites and the Making of Islamic Society* (New York, 2007, pb. edn 2011)

Kulka, Otto Dov, *Landscapes of the Metropolis of Death* (Cambridge, MA, 2013)

Lacquer, Thomas, *The Work of the Dead: A Cultural History of Mortal Remains* (Princeton, NJ, 2015)

Linkman, Audrey, *Photography and Death* (London, 2011)

Llewellyn, Nigel, *The Art of Death: Visual Culture in the English Death Ritual, c. 1500–c. 1800* (London, 1991)

Margolit, Avishai, *The Ethics of Memory* (Cambridge, MA, 2002)

Ruby, Jay, *Secure the Shadow: Death and Photography in America* (Cambridge, MA, 1995)

Scheffler, Samuel, *Death and the Afterlife* (Oxford, 2013)

Sebald, W. G., *Campo Santo* (New York, 2005)

Sorabji, Richard, *Self: Ancient and Modern Insights about Individuality, Life, and Death* (Chicago, IL, 2006)

Teresi, Dick, *The Undead* (New York, 2012)

The Tibetan Book of the Dead, trans. Gyurme Dorje (London, 2005)

Acknowledgements

Sandy Greene, who transformed my handwritten manuscript into typed print and then conveyed it electronically to the publisher; Alan N. Stone and Lesley Hill, who volunteered free access to their visual images; Harry Gilonis, who successfully pursued images required by the book; the generations of graduate students at Columbia who persevered successfully in my seminars on ancient death rituals, sarcophagi and related monuments; the owners of copyright protection of texts and images who made them available by permission; and to my wife Eleanor, indefatigable conveyor of emails and relevant bits of the Internet, for her unflagging, affectionate support.

Thank you.

Permissions

'Once I'm Dead' taken from *Family Values* by Wendy Cope (London: Faber & Faber, 2011), © Wendy Cope and reprinted by permission of Faber & Faber

'The Apparition' from *The Stairwell* by Michael Longley (London: Jonathan Cape, 2014), © Michael Longley 2014

'The Children's Memorial at Yad Vashem' from *The Holy Worm of Praise* by Philip Schultz is copyright © 2002 by Philip Schultz and reprinted by permission of Georges Borchardt, Inc., for Philip Schultz

'A Clear Day and No Memories' and 'As You Leave the Room' taken from *Collected Poems* by Wallace Stevens (London: Faber & Faber, 2006), © Estate of Wallace Stevens and reprinted by permission of Faber & Faber

'A Congo Funeral' from *A Map of the Night* by David Wagoner (Champaign, Illinois: University of Illinois Press, 2008) is copyright © 2008 by David Wagoner, used with permission of the poet and the University of Illinois Press

Photo Acknowledgements

The author and publishers wish to express their thanks to the below sources of illustrative material and/or permission to reproduce it. Some locations of artworks are also given below, in the interests of brevity. Every effort has been made to contact copyright holders; should there be any we have been unable to reach or to whom inaccurate acknowledgements have been made please contact the publishers, and full adjustments will be made to any subsequent printings.

Archaeological Museum, Zagreb: p. 51 (top); photos by or courtesy of the author: pp. 6, 16, 17, 20, 21, 35, 39, 43, 45, 49, 50, 51, 53, 58, 65, 74, 81, 84, 85, 91, 93, 94, 98, 100, 101, 105, 108 (top), 109, 110 (right), 113, 114, 115 (lower left and lower right), 122, 127, 130, 131, 140, 141, 144, 145, 147, 160, 175, 176 (top left and top right), 178 (top), 180, 182, 183; Basel Minster, Switzerland: p. 39; Basilica Cattedrale Patriarcale di San Marco, Venice (Baptistery): p. 108 (top); Basilica di San Vitale, Ravenna: p. 144 (top); Basilica di Santa Croce, Florence: pp. 54, 78 (lower right), 131; Basilica di Santa Sabina all'Aventino, Rome: p. 130; Basilica dei Santi Giovanni e Paolo, Rome: p. 175; 'basilica sotterranea di Porta Maggiore', Rome: p. 178 (top); photo © Nicole Bengiveno/ *New York Times*, Redux/eyevine: p. 48; Biblioteca Apostolica, Rome: p. 170; Bibliothèque Nationale, Paris: pp. 107, 127; from Govard Bidloo, *Anatomia humani corporis centum et quinque tabulis … illustrata …* (Amsterdam, 1685): p. 115 (lower left); from Robert Blair, *The Grave,*

A Poem: Illustr[ated] by 12 etchings executed ... from the Orig[inal] Designs (of W[illiam] Blake) (London, 1808): p. 176 (foot); photo H. Brandenburg: p. 97; British Museum, London: pp. 15, 75, 185; Bro Church, Gotland, Sweden: p. 176 (top left); Camposanto Monumentale, Pisa: p. 53; photo © 2007 Graham Claytor – published by the Institute for the Study of the Ancient World as part of the Ancient World Image Bank (AWIB): p. 18; from Francesco Colonna, *Hypnerotomachia Poliphili, ubi humana omnia non nisi somnium esse docet ...* (Venice, 1499): p. 23; Cooper Hewitt, Smithsonian Design Museum, New York: p. 154 (right); Coptic Museum, Cairo: p. 92; photo Dsdugan: p. 89; Duomo di Orvieto: p. 181; Duomo di Parma (Baptistery): p. 144 (foot); from Max Ernst, *Une Semaine de bonté* (Paris, 1934); © ADAGP, Paris and DACS, London 2017: pp. 121, 133; courtesy eyevine, London: p. 48; from Gabriele Faerno, *Fabulae centum ex antiquis auctoribus delectae et a Gabriele Faerno Cremonensi carminibus explicatae* (Rome, 1564): p. 136; Galerie der Stadt Stuttgart (© DACS 2017): p. 120; Galleria degli Uffizi, Florence: p. 142; from Jacques Gamelin, *Nouveau receuil d'ostéologie et de myologie dessiné après nature ... pour l'utilité des sciences et des arts ...* (Toulouse, 1779): p. 122; Gaziantep Arkeoloji Müzesi, Turkey: p. 171; photo Inductiveload: p. 164; İstanbul Arkeoloji Müzeleri (Istanbul Archaeological Museum): p. 80; photo Jastrow: p. 139; photo JoJan: p. 181; Kunsthaus, Zürich: p. 91; Kunstmuseum, Basel: p. 117; photo Lop Nur: p. 28 (top); Manchester City Art Galleries: p. 98; photo Masur: p. 142; Metropolitan Museum of Art, New York: pp. 32, 153; Minneapolis Institute of Art: p. 163; photo Morgan Library, New York: p. 112 (right); Musée Archéologique de Lamta, Tunisia: p. 51 (foot); Musée des Beaux Arts, Nantes: p. 103; Museo Civico Archeologico Oreste Nardini, Velletri: pp. 150, 151; Musée Gustave Moreau, Paris: pp. 148, 156; Musée du Louvre, Paris: pp. 77, 141; Musées Royaux des Beaux Arts de Belgique, Brussels: p. 159; Musei Capitolini, Rome: p. 86 (top); Museo del Alcázar de los Reyes Cristianos, Córdoba: p. 152; Museo Archeologico Nazionale, Naples: pp. 76 (top), 112 (left); Museo Archeologico Nazionale di Paestum:

pp. 76 (foot), 174; Museo delle Arti Decorative, Castello Sforzesco, Milan: p. 154 (left); Museo Nazionale Romano, Rome: pp. 110 (left), 139; Museo Nazionale Romano – Palazzo Massimo, Rome: p. 178 (foot); Museo del Vaticano, Rome: pp. 56 (foot), 146, 158, 173, 188; National Gallery of Australia, Canberra: p. 28 (foot); National Museum of Beirut, Lebanon: p. 87; photo National Park Service Digital Image Archives: p. 90; photo Petrusbarbygere: p. 179; Pinacoteca di Brera, Milan: p. 86 (foot); private collections: pp. 88 (reproduced courtesy of the artist, Dana Schutz, and Petzel, New York), 183; reproduced courtesy of the artist (Rosamund Purcell): p. 126; Rheinisches Landes-museum, Bonn: p. 56 (top); Römanisches-Germanisches Museum, Köln: p. 19; San Giovanni, Florence (Baptistery): p. 145 (left); Santa Maria Novella, Florence: p. 104; Santo Tome, Toledo: p. 179; Scheringa Museum of Realist Art, Spanbroek, Netherlands (© Paul Delvaux Foundation – St Idesbald/DACS 2017): p. 106; photo Shakko: p. 102; Edward Sorel/*New Yorker* © Condé Nast: p. 42; State Hermitage Museum, St Petersburg: p. 78 (lower left); State Pushkin Museum, Moscow: p. 102; The Tate, London: pp. 79, 118; from [Andreas Vesalius], *Andreæ Vesalii suorum De humani corporis fabrica librorum epitome* (Basel, 1543): p. 115 (lower right); Via Tor di Nona, Rome: p. 43; Victoria and Albert Museum, London: p. 73; photo Leonard Von Matt: p. 57; whereabouts unknown: pp. 35, 74, 78 (top), 100, 105, 108 (top), 109.

Graham Claytor has published the image on p. 18 online under conditions imposed by a Creative Commons Attribution 2.0 Generic license; Ahubling at English Wikipedia has published the image on p. 59 online under conditions imposed by a Creative Commons Attribution 3.0 Unported license; Gmihail at Serbian Wikipedia has published the image on p. 116 online, under conditions imposed by a Creative Commons Attribution-Share Alike 3.0 Serbia license;

Andrzej Otrębski has published the image on the lower left of p. 78 online, Jojan that on p. 181 online, Michel wal that on p. 152 online, Robby Robinette that on pp. 26–7 online, and Thelmadatter that on p. 123 online, under conditions imposed by a Creative Commons Attribution-Share Alike 3.0 Unported license; Wellcome Images have published the image at the top of p. 115 online under conditions imposed by a Creative Commons Attribution 4.0 International license; Tomascastelazohas published the image on p. 124 online, under conditions imposed by a Creative Commons Attribution-Share Alike 3.0 Unported license, a 2.5 Generic license, a 2.0 Generic license and a 1.0 Generic license; readers are free to share – to copy, distribute and transmit these works – or to remix – to adapt these works under the following conditions: they must attribute the work(s) in the manner specified by the author or licensor (but not in any way that suggests that they endorse you or your use of the work(s)) and if they alter, transform, or build upon the work(s), they may distribute the resulting work(s) only under the same or similar licenses to those listed above.

Index

Page numbers in *italic* refer to illustrations.